Two Wrongs
Don't Make a Right
...It Makes Us Even

Kennedee Devoe

Devoe Publications

This book is an original idea written by Kennedee Devoe. No parts of this book shall be duplicated, reproduced, or shared without the writer's permission. By reading this book, you are agreeing to such terms.

***No real names or precise fact patterns have been used to protect the privacy of the parties involved. ***

Written and created by Kennedee Devoe
Editor: Jill Duska
Cover designed: Donna Osborn Clark
Layout and Interior designed by: Devoe Publicatons

Published by: Devoe Publications
ISBN-13: 978-0989987103
ISBN-10: 0989987108

My book is dedicated to my dad and grandfathers may their souls rest in paradise. I know you are looking down smiling and are so proud of me. I love you!

If you haven't been in a few bad relationships, then this probably isn't the book for you.

~Kennedee Devoe~

Acknowledgments

I would like to thank God for keeping me blessed and focused. Although there are a few cuss words in here, it doesn't mean I love Him any less. I'm still a work in progress. I would like to say I love my "mama", aka my grandmother Ms. King. I get my feistiness from you. You and Dad raised me, and I thank you for always encouraging me to aim high. I would like to thank my biological mom Twyla for all her support over the years. I have a huge family, so I won't thank every single person, but thanks to my aunts, uncles, sister, brothers, nieces, nephew, and cousins for all your love and support. Special thanks to my aunts Tania, Terrayne, Ellen, Kelley, and my uncles Pete, Lenice, Darrell, Dez, and Mark. Thanks to my surrogates, aka my godparents Sheila and Moe. You all have always been there for me and I truly appreciate it. My career mentor Carolyn, you have helped me in every way. Thanks to my companion for the last four years for loving me just as I am, flaws and all. I would like to thank all my friends (my ride or dies) who have been there for the good, bad, and everything in between. I love you all like family, and I appreciate the loyalty that we share in our circle. Lastly, I would like to thank everyone that has supported me in this endeavor. I truly, truly appreciate it. If I forgot to thank anyone, please charge it to my head and not my heart.

I would like to acknowledge the following individuals for their role in assisting me with this book.

Stacy Brandy Johnson and Rochelle Howard for mentoring me.

Nia Black, Debra Lane, and Stephanie Nixon
for critiquing my work before anyone else laid eyes on it.

Jill Alicea for your part in helping get this book together.

Prologue

I t's funny how life takes us through so many changes. Those changes can either make or break you as a person. I have dated many men in my lifetime. I would say the majority of them broke my heart with their lies, cheating, and deception. After many failed relationships, I decided that it was time for the men to feel some type of sorrow for their actions. I've had men in my family like my Uncle Lee, my cousin Derwin, and my gang-affiliated Triple, Triple OG cousin DJ to put hands on the men that have truly disrespected me. However, I wanted men to understand that they couldn't treat me just any kind of way and get away with it. I wanted to fight my own battles for men to understand that I was a force to be reckoned with. I came up with creative ways to seek vengeance and cause sorrow to the men that attempted to use me, lie to me, and cheat on me. I had come to believe that men no longer valued women, but held their material possessions on a pedestal, and this would be the key to causing them as much sorrow as they did to me. Don't get me wrong, I'm no gangbanger, hood chick, or bad ass. However, what I am is a fighter.

When I say I am a fighter, I do not mean in terms of actually fighting. It means that I will never allow anyone to hurt me, take advantage of me, mistreat me, or disrespect me, and let them think that it's all right. The bottom line is, I'm going to treat you how you treat me. Every man I would meet would all be different yet the same in the patterns that they exhibited at the end of the relationship. As for me, I created a pattern that only I could I break when I was ready.

Mashon – How It All Started

My parents allowed me to start accepting phone calls and visits from boys when I was fifteen. I met a boy named Mashon. He seemed to be a bit of a nerd, but he was cute. He was sixteen with a driver's license and his own car. We started off talking on the phone, and because of his geekiness, he was very helpful in getting my math homework done. We would go on dates to the movies, McDonald's, and his high school basketball games.

The time that we were spending together seemed to be going well between the two of us until one evening he showed up at my doorstep with another girl. I had no clue what the hell was going on. When I opened my front door, there he stood on the porch with a smirk on his face. The girl with him stood about six feet tall, and he was only five feet nine. She had her arms crossed with an angry look on her face. He told me that this was his new girlfriend and he didn't want to be my boyfriend anymore.

I was crushed that he had just broken up with me and that he had the audacity to bring his new girlfriend with him to break the news. My mom taught me to always be a lady. However, my first impulse when those words left his mouth was to scratch his eyes out. Instead of acting on it, I just closed the door in his face. I went to my room and called my friends to tell them what had happened.

Each person I told this story to that night sat on the phone in disbelief. It's okay to break up with someone, but the way it was done was the gut buster. I just have to reiterate how hurt I was, and I wanted him to feel that same exact hurt. So, I plotted with my girls how I would get my revenge.

A few weeks later, the plan was executed by toilet papering and spraying shaving cream on his car and his parent's house. The next day, Mashon called my mother to let her know he thought I had vandalized his car and parent's home. One thing that I learned about my mother was that even if she thought I was wrong, she would never let the other person know that I was. My mother told Mashon that she was sorry to hear that, and she hoped he caught the person who was responsible, but that it wasn't me.

When my mother hung up the phone, she said, "No telephone for a week, and don't even think about going nowhere."

I didn't even have to ask why. I knew, and she knew as well, that I was guilty. I thought to myself, *This boy is such a punk for telling my mother on me.*

Later that week, I snuck on the phone and called Mashon. When he picked up the phone, I said, "I am going to kick your ass!" and then I hung up.

He immediately called back. My mother answered. He told her what I had said. My mother said, "Kennedee is on phone restriction, so I don't think she called you." Little did my mother know I had used the cordless phone in the bathroom and snuck it back on the charger before she realized it was missing.

When you are younger, it seems like a week of punishment is like an eternity in jail. That week of isolation made me wonder how my situation with Mashon turned sour. The only answer that I came up with was that he was a jerk.

By that Friday, I had persuaded my mother to allow me to go to the high school basketball game. She agreed. I was there with my girls, Dani and Rachel, and they ran with a group of boys who called themselves the Tow Up Posse. Posses were popular back then. However, looking back on it, they were nothing but preppy guys in a gang.

On that night, I was glad to be with them. There was a sense of safety knowing that I was rolling with a crew of fifteen guys. After the game, all of us went to Denny's to eat. I was cornered by Mashon while coming out of the bathroom. I was hotter than fish grease.

He told me, "I'm going to fuck you up for messing up my car and my parent's house!"

I asked him, "How do you know I even had anything to do with that?"

His voice went into a higher pitch as he yelled, "Because I do!"

Luckily, one of the guys from the posse saw what was going on and came to my rescue. Consequently, after we all ate, Mashon confronted us while coming out of the restaurant with his six-man posse in the parking lot. You do the math: six guys to fifteen guys just wasn't going to be a good outcome. Mashon got all in my face, screaming about the same topic that he had just asked me about. At that moment, the way everyone was standing felt like it was the Michael Jackson "Bad" video. All the guys seemed like they were just waiting for someone to make the wrong move, and it was going to be on.

Looking back at this situation, I am glad that the only person who did get hurt was Mashon. It was me who threw the first punch. I balled my fist up and hit him right in the jaw. He was so busy talking that he didn't even see it coming. I hit him so hard that his glasses flew to the ground. The next thing I know, this guy named Jesse from the Tow Up Posse picked me up and put me in Rachel's car. It was in my best interest because Mashon was hot that he had just gotten sucker-punched by a girl. How embarrassed he must have been at that moment to get hit by me in front of all his boys.

For weeks, the talk of the neighborhood was how Mashon got knocked out by me. People exaggerate the truth. I just said I hit him and knocked off his glasses. I said nothing about knocking him out. However, this was the story and the legend that followed me for many years. When I hit him that night, it was exactly what I felt like doing that night when he showed up on my porch with that girl. It was a great feeling. I was exhilarated. This thing called consequences and repercussions… who would have thought I would have done something like that? I walked around for months feeling untouchable until one summer afternoon.

I was taking a walk in the neighborhood when Mashon caught me off guard. He pulled his car over and got out of the car. He never even said a word. He just got out and pushed me to the ground. When I tried to get up, he kicked me in my ass. At that point, I just stayed down and began to cry. Now don't get me wrong, I wasn't crying because I had just skinned my elbow or because my ass was sore, but because I was angry. I just couldn't believe that this was happening to me.

Once I started crying, he ran to his car and drove off. I had to walk back home, which was like five blocks away, with my ass hurting.

As I walked in the door, my mother noticed me limping. She asked with a strain in her voice, "What happened to you?"

I explained to her what Mashon had done and what had caused the situation.

She just looked at me like I was crazy and said, "Go to your room."

My family never kept me in the loop about everything, but about a week later, I overheard my Uncle Lee, Aunt Tia, and mom discussing how my uncle had discovered where Mashon lived. He explained that he had found Mashon outside playing basketball. He asked Mashon if he knew his niece Kennedee. When Mashon heard my name, he tried to run. My uncle caught him and threw him in the rose bushes, and when Mashon tried to get up, he kicked him in the ass. My uncle said he told Mashon that he better not have any more problems out of him.

To my surprise, I heard my mom and uncle start to laugh. To a certain extent, I felt bad for Mashon, but on the other hand, he started all this mess. All he had to do was break up with me over the phone like a true gentle-man rather than show up on my doorstep with his new girlfriend. It was crazy how something so small was the beginning of a spiral of actions of bigger things to come.

~~~

All my life, all I have ever hoped for was finding a man who was loving, honest, faithful, sincere, supportive, understanding, caring, affectionate, spiritual, compas-sionate, a good listener, respectful, and goal-oriented. Get the picture? Every girl/woman wants to find a man who has certain qualities about himself that make you want to spend the rest of your life with him.

Unfortunately, I have met so many men disguised as Mr. Right that turned out to be Mr. Wrong. There have been so many scenarios that I can speak of, like the time this guy punched me in the mouth. I was hit so hard that I fell to the ground and hit my head on the curb. The next thing I remember was me waking up at my homegirl's house asking what happened. Or the time some guy took me on a double date and left me and my girl Serena while we were in the bathroom. Or the time this guy decided to drag race down Crenshaw, passing through all the red lights, and then getting mad at me for asking him to take me home. Instead, he let me out on Imperial and Crenshaw and socked me in my back while I got out of the car. Or the guy who tried to strangle me with the seatbelt because we got into an argument. Honestly, these are real stories that could go on and on. I have so many that it was difficult for me to decide which ones I'd share in this book. So allow me to introduce you to the men who made me the woman I was and the woman I am now.

Royce – Love Isn't Supposed To Hurt

Back in the day, Crenshaw was a popping spot. All you needed was a fly ride and a full tank of gas, and that was your Sunday night. People would cruise up and down Crenshaw for hours, flossing and getting numbers. For the fellas, it was harder for them to get numbers if their ride was a bucket. However, for the ladies, it didn't matter what you were driving as long as you were fly in the face or had a banging body. If you had a combination of the two, you probably would be getting a whole lot more numbers than the average young girl. Crenshaw was my Sunday hang-out spot. You could meet a guy cruising on Sunday, and by Friday, he was your new boyfriend.

Well, I found this guy named Royce. He was nineteen and I was eighteen. He was tall with a medium build, and he reminded me of a chocolate-brown version of Tupac. Royce had a daughter, and she was two years old. That was the first time that I had dated anyone with a child. He seemed responsible and he took care of her. His baby mama was a little older; she was twenty-two. He said they weren't together because she wasn't a good mother. I figured if his attitude was like that towards her, I probably wouldn't have any problems with him trying to get back together with her.

Things were cool at first. We would go out to dinner, movies, bowling, and miniature golfing. We even attended each other's family events. We had gotten so close that he started going to church with me. We both were making decent money even though we were youngsters. Some weekends, we got a room at a nice hotel and just relaxed and enjoyed one another.

These adventures eventually led to us having sex and me getting pregnant. When I first discovered that I was pregnant, he seemed happy. However, as the months progressed, his demeanor began to change. We were no longer going out as much. Back then, we had pagers, not cell phones, and my pages weren't getting returned as often as they used to. He became M.I.A.

After so many episodes of him missing, I decided just to do my own thing. However, I realized that you can't really do your own thing when you're pregnant. I was at work when I met a guy who was about 6'2", bald, and chocolate like an Easter bunny. He reminded me of Malik Yoba, minus the ashy lips. His name was Garin, and he was twenty-three. He asked me for my number, and I wrote it down on a piece of paper.

He looked at the paper and said, "Nice penmanship."

I thought, *Geesh, that was corny!* I watched him stroll over to a red 525 BMW. I was turned off immediately. Back then, guys with nice cars were deemed players, and I was having enough trouble with Royce without having to add to the drama.

When Garin called, he and I had the basic conversation of how many kids, relationship status, and occupation. He told me that he was single, no children, and a music producer. I was turned off again when he said he was a music producer. In the 90's, it seemed like everyone was in the "studio" and was a "producer". He then flipped the script on me, and asked me the same questions. I informed him that I was pregnant.

"You sure didn't look pregnant," said Garin.

I replied, "Well, I am."

He replied, "That's not a problem. What's up with you and your baby daddy?"

I said, "He is still in the picture, but things are iffy."

He said, "Cool! Would you like to go out?"

Even though I wasn't pleased with his car and his occupation, I thought, *What the hell, why not?*

Garin and I went out to Fridays in the Marina. We had a good time. It turned out that he actually was a high-profile producer, and he really was in the studio. I still wasn't impressed. Someone like that was bound to have a million video-type girls at his beck and call. I was a pretty girl, but I didn't have a lot of physical attributes below the neck that would make a guy say, "Damn, she bad!" So instead of putting myself through more heartache, I decided to put Garin in the friend category. Plus, I was still pregnant.

Garin turned out to be a true gentleman despite my circumstances. This made me realize that I wasn't ready to have a child with Royce. I was four months pregnant at the time when my car had a flat tire. I called him to ask if he could come over to put the spare on. He came right over, but acted as if he didn't want to be there. He expected me to help him change the tire. He said I needed to learn how to change a tire. There I was, standing there pregnant with his baby, and he wanted to show me how to change a freakin' tire. I was floored. As I stood there, he actually tried to tell me how to do it, and then he had the nerve to hand me one of the tools.

I was in my second trimester. I knew I didn't want a baby after that, and definitely not with him. I made an appointment at the abortion clinic to terminate the pregnancy. The abortion was a two-day procedure. The first day, Royce and I went together and the doctor inserted cervical dilators. It wasn't painful until I left the clinic. My stomach started to cramp something awful. I had the urge to go to the bathroom about twenty times. Once the pain started to go away, I was able to gather my composure and write a letter to my mother explaining where I was and what I was doing. When I woke up that morning, I said bye to my mother and left the note on the kitchen counter. I met Royce at his house and we drove together to the clinic.

I couldn't eat a thing until after the procedure. Royce knew this, yet he went to the corner liquor store and bought some chips and began munching on them right in front of me. I was starving like an Ethiopian orphan, and there he was getting his eat on. I could have choked him right then and there.

They finally took me in about an hour later after my appointment time. They did an ultrasound, took blood work, and then had me sit in the waiting room for another thirty minutes. I was finally led into a room that had a medical bed with stirrups at the end of the table. I lay down on the table, a needle was inserted in my arm with an anesthesia, and after that it was all a blur.

When I woke up, I was sore and bleeding very heavily. They gave me juice and crackers, then called Royce's name to meet in the hallway. When I got in the hallway, there was Royce with his black self standing there with a stupid look on his face.

"How are you feeling?" mumbled Royce.

I fired back, "How do you think I am feeling?" I was so angry with myself and was so angry with him.

Afterwards, Royce and I rented a hotel room. I was in so much pain, and he was getting on my nerves because he was still being a jerk. I was hungry, tired, and feeling bad about my decision. This man had the nerve to ask me to give him some oral sex because I couldn't have regular sex. I was so outdone with him. I had just had this procedure done, and all his ass could do was think about getting his rocks off. When I refused, he mistreated me for the remainder of the night.

I went home the next morning. I made sure I came home after I knew that my dad had already left for work. When I arrived back at home, my mom was in the kitchen sitting at the counter. She wasn't as upset as I thought she would be. I had been sure that my mom was going to kill me with her bare hands. We were from a Christian background. It was bad enough I had fornicated then gotten pregnant out of wedlock, but to top it off, I committed murder by having an abortion.

To my surprise, my mother didn't yell at me. She hugged me and asked me how I felt. I never truly shared what happened, but I told her I was fine. That procedure took a lot out of me; I was on bed rest for three days. My breasts begin to swell, harden, and leak milk. I was very uncomfortable and still in pain. I went to my mother. I told her how I was feeling. She got an old sheet, ripped it up, and began wrapping the sheet around my breasts. She said it would help with the swelling and leakage.

I had promised myself that I wasn't going to deal with Royce after the way he treated me. However, he called me every day to see how I was doing. I kept the conversations short and sweet, as I was trying to gradually leave him alone.

About five days after the abortion, I received a phone call from Royce's baby mama. Her name was Syleena. She told me that she found pictures of Royce and me. She had gone through his pager and found my number. She wanted to know who I was. I explained to her that I would consider myself his ex-girlfriend. I told her how long he and I had been a couple. I also explained to her all the events that had led to us no longer being together, including my abortion.

She shared that this wasn't his first time cheating on her. This is when I realized the whole time he was seeing me, he was still with her. I had been played. I could understand to a certain extent his bipolar personality and all his MIA's. Syleena said I wasn't the first girl he had gotten pregnant either; he actually had two other children by two other women. I was baffled.

Syleena had this bright idea to confront Royce face-to-face together. I agreed to the idea. Because I didn't know her well, I asked my friend Rachel to accompany me. Rachel and I picked up Syleena from her job because she didn't have a car, and we went over to Royce's house. He was only expecting her to come, but to his surprise, I was there too.

Syleena and I both got out of the car, Rachel waited in the passenger seat. Syleena and I began questioning him about his cheating ways. All he could do was stand there and look stupid. He had no answers to our questions. I called him a sorry motherfucker, and out of all the things said that day, he got mad at that.

He finally decided to open his mouth just to call me a lying bitch. He grabbed me by my ears. Then I heard him making this loud sound in his throat, and out came the biggest blob of spit I had ever seen. He grabbed me by my ears and the spit landed directly in my face.

That did it! That was the highest form of disrespect. I got so angry that I kicked my leg far behind me to swing it back to the front and give him the kick of a lifetime, right in the balls.

My hit landed right in the dick. I heard him say, "Oh, shit!"

I got so engrossed in seeing his reaction that I didn't see that he was getting ready to hit me with his closed left fist. His fist connected to my left eye and the top of my nose. The impact of the hit was so hard that I slid, fell to the ground, and ripped the knees of my pants. Syleena and Rachel start yelling and screaming at him. I was bleeding profusely from my eye. They both helped me into the passenger side of my car. Rachel drove around the corner to a store and called 911.

We drove back around the corner to meet the police. The officer took Royce's and my statements. Royce claimed I hit him first; he wanted to press charges if I was going to press charges against him. I looked at the officer in awe, because there I was bleeding to death and that boy didn't have a scratch on him. The officer said we both could go to jail if we both pressed charges against each other.

I said to forget it then. I knew it would kill my mom to have to come get me out of jail. As I walked away and got back into the car, Royce was standing there with a smirk on his face. He thought he had gotten off scot-free after assaulting me. Oh boy, oh boy, would he be wrong!

Syleena and Rachel drove me to the emergency room. They admitted me very quickly because my eye was still bleeding profusely. The outcome of the emergency room visit was fifteen stitches and a broken nose. All that from one hit.

Afterwards, Rachel dropped Syleena off at her job and we then headed back to my house. When I walked in the house, the look on my mother's face was of horror. Her look was of a broken-hearted mother who knew her daughter was hurt.

I explained everything that had happened. I was off from work for a week because I had to get my broken nose fixed. I couldn't breathe through my nose; I had to breathe through my mouth, which caused dehydration. He hit a nerve in my eye that made my vision sensitive to light. I walked around with sunglasses on in the house for days. I eventually had to go back to the doctor. My eye was dilated and the sensitivity issue was resolved. My black eye healed very slowly. It turned various shades, from red to purple to green, and finally black. I walked around for weeks ashamed of what had happened. Never did I think that this situation could or would have escalated to this. The meeting with Syleena and Royce was supposed to expose him for his lying and wrongdoings not turn into the Ike and Tina Revue.

Eventually, word got around the neighborhood about what had happened to me. Many of my male friends offered to go "handle" the situation for me. I declined. A co-worker called and said her uncle was a sheriff, and she had told him about the situation. My co-worker's uncle came to my parent's house, and he took a report and pictures of my battered face. Royce was in the Highway Patrol Explorer program, and he was going to be a highway patrolman. My co-worker's uncle forwarded the report and pictures to the commander of the Explorer program. The commander, who turned out to be a female, contacted me for further information.

Royce was dismissed from the program and would never be eligible to work in law enforcement ever again. I was relieved that justice was done, at the cost of his career. After being terminated from the program, Royce called and threatened to kill me. I had no choice but to take his threat seriously, as he already had the nerve to hit me.

My mother made my uncles aware of the situation. My Uncle Lee, who had by then become a preacher, decided that he and a fellow minister from the church would go to Royce's job just to "talk" to him. I thought that was very amusing, since I knew there would be no talking involved. I was told that Royce declined the invitation to come outside and converse with my uncle and his friend.

Consequently, when Royce came out, he found his car wet. My uncle and his friend had poured paint thinner all over his fly ride. Unfortunately, this would not be the last of repercussions for Royce hitting me.

I had a friend coming from out of state to visit for the holidays, and I told him about the incident. He decided to go pick up his brother and go to Royce's job. Royce worked at night, which was a disadvantage for him because it would be dark when he came out to go home.

Royce was caught off guard by Brian and KC, and he received the ass-whipping that he indeed deserved. The next day, I received a call from Syleena informing me that Royce had got jumped at his job. I told her, "Oh well." I mean, what, did she really think that I was about to confirm to her that I had something to do with it? Royce contacted me one final time via phone to tell me he was going to kill me no matter what. All I could do was hang up the phone then quickly pick it up again to call PAC Bell to change my telephone number.

I shared with my parents the conversation Royce had with me, and they decided it was best that I pack my bags and be sent out of town. I left for Atlanta three days later. I was sad that I had to leave all my family and friends behind. I left with no job in sight, no family, and no direction. I was only financially stable due to some money that I had inherited. I moved into an already-furnished apartment paying $425 a month with all utilities paid. My dad drove my car down a week later. I finally had transportation.

However, it wasn't easy living in a new state where I didn't know anyone. All of my girls and my family would call me and write me to let me know that they hadn't forgotten about me. I didn't receive any mail from Garin, but he sure did call frequently to make sure that I was okay. I didn't have much of a social life. However, I did find work.

My first job was as a telemarketer for an alarm company. I sold zero alarms, and within a month, I was fired. That was the first job I was ever fired from. My second job was at BP gas station, where I worked as a cashier for two months. I ended up quitting there because they had me working nights, and that just didn't seem safe to me. I ended working my last few months at Kroger, which was a grocery store. I already had experience in the grocery retail industry so I started off as a cashier, and within a month, I was a floor manager. I was finally glad to have found a better-paying job, but I was miserable and homesick.

After eight months of hiding, I returned to California. It took me two days to drive back home and $60 worth of shipping to get my belongings back to California. I was glad to be home with family and friends.

My first few weeks back, I was a little paranoid. I was so afraid that I was going to run into Royce and that his last words to me would become true. It would be almost two years before Royce and I crossed paths again.

It was September 1994. I was at a beauty shop in Long Beach. He walked in when I was getting my hair done. Luckily, my stylist was nearly finished with me when his eyes finally found me across the room and stared at me like they were darts. When my hair was done I calmly got up and walked to the exit, and we exchanged the evil eye at one another. In the back of my mind, I was waiting for him to get up, follow me to the parking lot, and kill me right there. However, the evil eye was all I received.

I was so glad it went down like that. I guess after the backlash he received, that is all that he had better have done was give me the evil eye. After all, I didn't deserve him putting his hands on me. Even years later, I still feel the effects of his hit. I lost a little hearing in my left ear. Every now and then, my eye decides to water for no reason due to a nerve he hit in my eye. Man, he must have been He-Man that day, cause he used all his might to try and knock me out. All of this came from one hit. What a shame!

Ryan – All Eyez on Me

After Royce, I started to believe that maybe dating older men would be the answer to my solution. I started to see Garin, but I just couldn't take him seriously. Garin and I had finally taken our friendship to the next level; we slept together. It was a lil more than what I bargained for. I could tell he was too experienced for my taste. He wanted for us to do it 69, for me to ride his dick backward, and he was into S & M. The sex was a bit too much for my taste. He didn't like that I was still a lil girl in the bedroom. I was twenty years old, yet he wanted me to be a porno star. I definitely wasn't on his sexual level. So instead of pursuing Garin, I decided to set my sights elsewhere.

I was at a gas station on Crenshaw when I met Ryan. Ryan hopped out of his black Chevy SS, and I liked what I saw. My preference always has been tall men, because I am 5'7" myself. He stood about 6'2" inches, just how I like, medium build, smooth mocha skin, and a very nice smile. He made his way over to my car and asked me for my name and number. I gladly gave it to him. He called the next day, and we talked for hours. Ryan was twenty-eight years old with two little boys. I never had dated anyone that much older than myself, plus he had two kids, which made me very skeptical. Dealing with one kid is a little different, but two kids? And they were only two years apart in age? This made me very reluctant.

Instead of following my first instinct, I went ahead and said I would go out with him. He drove sixty miles just to take me out on our first date. Unfortunately, I had to find a friend to bring along because he was bringing one of his friends. So I asked my friend Adrian to go, and she agreed. Ryan and his friend Frankie came to pick me up, and we went to go pick up Adrian. We went to the bowling alley, but Adrian wasn't feeling Frankie, so the date was cut short.

Ryan asked me on a second date, and I accepted. He drove down, but this time we went to the movies. The movie was horrible, and I was ready to go, as I was sitting there enduring a horrible storyline. Suddenly, his pager began vibrating every two minutes.

I politely said, "Maybe you should go call whoever that is back."

It wasn't until the sixth page that he decided to go call the person back. We both walked into the theater lobby for him to use the public pay phone. I stood at a distance, pretending to give him some privacy.

The conversation he was having sounded more like an interrogation. The conversation was something like, "What's up? Why? That's none of your business. I don't know. Bye." When he hung up the phone, he lowered his head and slowly, he said, "That was my baby mama calling me about the boys."

I said, "Okay. I'm ready to go."

Before we left, we both went into the restrooms. When we came out, a theater employee was standing by the pay phone with the receiver in his hand, saying, "Are you Ryan? Your wife is on the phone."

I was stunned that Ryan's baby mama turned out to be his wife. Ryan hesitantly approached the phone, and the employee handed him the receiver. He just took the receiver in his hand and hung it up. The employee explained, "I heard the phone ringing after I saw you using the phone, Sir, so I answered the phone. The lady on the line wanted to know where the phone booth was located, what city it was in, and to describe anyone that was with the person using the phone. I did answer all information that was requested. My apologies, Sir."

I could tell that Ryan was upset, but he calmly said, "Don't worry about it, kid."

We proceeded to walk to the car. He said, "Please let me explain." When we got in the car, he quickly said, "Yes, I am married, but we are separated right now. I have been married five years. Things weren't working out, and I plan on getting a divorce."

I'm sure some of us have heard this same line when a married man gets busted. However, his words turned out to be true. After only three months of dating, Ryan and I moved into a one-bedroom apartment. My mother told me that if I moved out with Ryan, I couldn't return home. I didn't think too much of it because I figured it would be all good between us.

Boy was I WRONG! We signed a one-year lease, paying $625 a month with all utilities included, with the exception of electricity. The only expenses that we had were his car note, both of our car insurance, food, cable bill, and personal expenses.

It wasn't too much longer before it felt like we were roommates instead of boyfriend and girlfriend. We were splitting the rent and bills 50/50. That was not what I had in mind when I moved out with him. Ryan would go out clubbing with his cousin, and he wouldn't come back until two or three in the morning. To top that off, his baby mama/wife would call and give me grief. She would call all times of the night, telling me to put her husband on the phone. One night, she got so bold to tell me that she was going to whip my ass when she saw me.

Don't get me wrong, this woman had a right to be angry, but not at me, because her marriage was already broken before I stepped on the scene. However, I knew that if I didn't nip her actions in the bud from the start, her threats wouldn't cease.

She didn't know I had been riding with Ryan coming to pick up the boys every weekend, which meant I knew where she lived. So I rounded up a few of my girls and we went to her house. I knocked on the door several times, and there was no answer, even though the lights were on. The girls stood outside talking shit, hoping she would come to the door so I could get that ass-whipping she promised. Unfortunately, she never came out. By the time I got back home, she had called and told Ryan. He wanted a reason why I did what I did.

"I wasn't going to have her calling our house disrespecting and threatening me," I explained.

He said, "I understand, but could you have handled it some other way?"

I looked at him and said, "No."

The conversation ended there. We changed the house number, and her method of contact was limited to her paging him.

She was the least of my problems with Ryan, because other problems inside of our relationship were beginning to escalate. Ryan's pager went off one night around 11:30 p.m. He acted as if he didn't hear it. In the back of mind, I knew something was up.

The next morning, I woke up, found the pager under the couch, and retrieved the number from it. When I got to work, I called the number back. I asked, "Did someone page Ryan?"

The female on the other end of the line replied, "Who is this, Kennedee?"

Startled, I said, "Yes! Who this is?"

"My name is Indigo. I know that you're Ryan's girl-friend. I was at your house last week," she said.

So I asked if she had been over to the house to describe it. She described it to a tee. She even knew that I had my Glamour Shots in picture frames on top of the entertainment center.

She said, "Ryan took down the pictures when I was there." I thought to myself, *I guess it is hard to cheat with a guilty conscience.* She went on to explain how she and Ryan had sex in our bed while I was at work. She told him that she didn't care that he had a girlfriend, because she just wanted to have sex.

At that point in the conversation, my ears couldn't stand to hear any more. I told her I had to go. I was at work, and I couldn't handle the situation like I needed. I hung up with her and I called him. When he picked up, I calmly said, "I need to ask you something."

"What?" he asked.

I asked, "Did you have a girl named Indigo over our house last week?"

He replied, "She had come over with my best friend Rick. Rick is the one who was messing with her."

I asked, "Why didn't you tell me that Rick had come by?"

He answered, "Because you were at work."

So I'm thinking to myself, *How stupid does he think I am?* All this time, Rick had never been to our house, and suddenly he comes over? Bullshit! I said, "You're lying! I'm on my way home!" I hung up the phone and I told my boss I wasn't feeling good, so I was leaving for the day.

During the thirty minute drive home, all I could do was think. Then I started to remember back to last week. That day when I had arrived home, he had all the windows open, airing out the house, burning incense, and he even cooked dinner that day. He was extra nice; I also remembered he had two scratches on his back. I remembered asking him about them, but he told me that he had received them while working out at the gym. I could feel myself getting angry because all the signs were there, and I had missed them all.

When I arrived at the house, he was nowhere to be found. I immediately picked up the phone and paged him over and over again. While waiting for his call, I started gathering his personal belongings and throwing them by the front door. I could hear my mother's voice in my head telling me I couldn't come back home if it didn't work out between Ryan and me. So I picked up all his things and placed them back in the closet. I figured I'd hear him out first. Seems crazy now, but I had nowhere to go. I needed him to help pay the rent.

He finally came back to the house about an hour later. I can remember us arguing, but I can't quite remember word for word what was said. However, I do remember finally getting tired of hearing all the lies regarding the situation come from his mouth. I just slapped the hell out of him, and in return, he slapped the hell out of me too. I fell to the floor.

He screamed, "Don't be putting your hands on me!"

I was in a state of shock that he had placed a hand on me. Furthermore, he wasn't even apologetic for what he did. I learned at an early age that you only bad mouth your significant other to your family when you know that you aren't going to work things out. Therefore, I only told my friends about the incident. I knew if I told my mom, then Ryan would have to pay the price for placing his hands on me.

I was on the edge with distrust for weeks. Every move Ryan made was being questioned, as I no longer trusted him. One evening while sitting in the house alone, still feeling insecure, I started to rummage through his clothes in the closet. I found a jacket pocket filled with little pieces of paper with women's names and numbers. I became infuriated, since one of the numbers matched with the area code of the city we lived in. I started thinking, and I began wondering if he had also brought her into our home. I quickly called the number on the paper. A woman picked up, and I asked her if she knew Ryan. She said she had met him at her job at the bowling alley. She explained that she had a boyfriend and had no intentions of talking with Ryan. I left it at that, and got off the phone with her.

I sat there with all those pieces of paper with telephone numbers on them and stared. Then I realized I couldn't live my life like this; it had to stop. When Ryan returned home, I sat him down, pulled out the pieces of paper, and began to cry. I explained that I wanted this to stop, because we had no choice but to work it out.

He held my hand, and finally apologized for his actions. He said he loved me, never meant to hurt me. He went into detail about why he felt he was cheating. He explained, "I married young and never really got a chance to date. Maybe I am compensating for lost time."

I showed no pity for his explanations. I just said, "Whatever the case may be, it ends now!"

He said it would, but somehow I just knew this wouldn't be the last time we had this discussion.

Our living situation was awkward. Months had passed. Ryan and I hadn't had sex. I just couldn't allow him to touch me after what he did. We would sleep in the same bed, but he knew not to touch me. This situation didn't last long. Ultimately, I ended up giving in.

From then on, everything seemed okay again between us. However, it wasn't long before he was running up in the clubs again with his cousin Myron. He would drive to LA to pick up Myron, head to the hottest clubs, and then come in at all times of the night. One evening, I decided I had enough of his club adventures.

I knew he was going out that night, so I cooked his favorite meal: steak, mashed potatoes, and green beans. I was so nice to him that evening. I fixed his plate with his favorite drink. I watched in amusement as he ate his favorite meal, and unknowingly washed it down with cranberry-grape juice spiked with milk of magnesia. I knew my concoction would work right about the time he hit the dance floor at the club.

Instead of his usual 3:00 a.m. arrival from the club, he arrived by midnight. I sat there on the couch watching TV. He burst into the door questioning if I felt ill too. I quietly laughed as he stumbled his way to the bathroom.

When he came out of the bathroom, he said, "My stomach has been hurting, and I have diarrhea."

I said, "That's odd, I feel just fine."

As he sat on the toilet for over twenty minutes I found myself laughing uncontrollably. He never figured out that I was the cause of his stomach troubles that night, but I took pure pleasure in knowing that I was the culprit.

Weeks passed and Ryan seemed to be content with staying home. But then the bug hit him again, and he was back out and about. I guess it's hard for a leopard to change his spots.

The first time that he went back out, he came home at a decent time. How ironic that his pager would go off the very next day. The pager started to go off around 1:00 in the morning. He did as he had previously when he was caught. He put the pager up underneath the couch.

I thought, *Did he not think I saw that?* Instead, I just played it off, and when he fell asleep, I was up underneath that couch looking for that pager. The next morning, I called the number back, and I wasn't surprised to find a woman's voice on the other line. She said that she had met Ryan at the club last night. She said that she had also asked Ryan if he had a girlfriend, and he told her no. I let her know that not only did he have a girlfriend, but that we lived together also. She told me that she did not mess with men who had other women in their lives and that I would have no problems with her ever calling him again. I didn't mention the call to Ryan, but I was upset for days.

Ryan's cousin Myron's birthday was coming up. Ryan told me he was taking him to Tijuana for the weekend. I was really displeased that he thought he could go away for a weekend and that I'd be all right with it. I just sat there and looked at him like he was dumb. He still went even though he knew I was not okay with him going on the trip.

During that weekend, he checked in periodically, but that still didn't ease my concerns. He returned from the trip trying to smooth the situation over by taking me to dinner. I got in the car, and a little voice said to let down the sun visor.

As soon as I pulled the sun visor down, two packs of condoms fell in my lap. I looked over at him with disgust. We never made it to dinner that night. We spent the entire night arguing about why he liked to cheat on me.

He swore up and down that nothing happened when he was in Tijuana. He claimed that the condoms were his cousin's. There was no reason for us to continue this discussion, because he was clearly lying, and all he did was upset me even more. After about three hours of going back and forth, I finally just walked into the bedroom and locked the door. Ryan spent several weeks on our couch.

Even though we were having trouble in our relationship, he was big on keeping up appearances with his family. Memorial Day weekend came around, and his family had their annual picnic at Puddingstone Park. We picked up his kids, and off to the park we went. His family was there, and there were lots of food and fun. I was trying to pretend to have a good time, but I just wasn't feeling the love between Ryan and me. I needed a break from the façade. I went to the car to sit for a while.

After about twenty minutes, I got out of the car and popped the trunk to get my sweater. As I closed the trunk, I heard a voice say, "Hi there, gorgeous."

I recognized the voice, but I thought to myself, *Naw, it couldn't be.* I turned around, and yep, it was. "Hey, Garin! Good to see you!"

He hopped out of his car and gave me a hug. He asked what I was doing up at the park. I told him I was there with my boyfriend's family. I asked him the same. He said he was there for one of the homey's picnics.

In the middle of the conversation, he stopped and said, "You know this guy?" I looked back, and there was Ryan, making his way to see what was going on.

Ryan finally made his way to the car. He grabbed me by the waist and asked, "Who's your friend?"

I said, "Ryan, this is Garin, Garin this is Ryan."

Garin turned to me and said, "Well, it's always good to see you. I'll get with you soon. Nice meeting you, Ryan. Take care of my girl."

I really hadn't been in contact with Garin since I had been with Ryan, since I was trying to be in a committed relationship with Ryan. After seeing him that day, I wondered if I had put him back in the friend zone too quickly. I guess I wasn't the only one wondering about Garin, because as soon as he drove off, Ryan began with the questions. Ryan wanted to know who Garin was, what did he mean by "my girl", what he was doing there, how I knew him, how long I knew him, and in what capacity? There were so many questions pertaining to Garin. It was funny to see the shoe on the other foot for once. The green-eyed bandit had arrived.

Weeks later, my patience was once again really getting tested by Ryan. He was getting on my nerves with his cheating ways and lying. To top it all off, he couldn't get enough of the club. Since I was only twenty, I decided to make use of my fake ID by hitting up some clubs with my best friend Taylor. We would get dressed in our party attire: sexy high heels, flawless makeup, and hair looking fly, then go out and have a good time. We went to hot clubs in LA like the Century Club, Tilly's Terrace, Golden Tail, Northern Lights, Savannah West, and some club in Irvine that I can't remember.

I would get approached by men when we went out. They would offer to buy drinks, take me out, and even inquire about taking me home for the night. I would pass on the drink and the one-night stand. However, I was interested in them taking me out. I was still living with Ryan, yet I just didn't feel loved by him any longer. Going out to the clubs and hearing men compliment me and want to do things for me helped with the self-esteem that was gradually dropping due to Ryan's cheating ways. Though I never made it out on any dates, I did indulge in phone conversations with some of these men that I met at the club.

I can remember one day when I came home and Ryan was sitting on the couch. I sat down next to him and he pulled out these tiny pieces of paper from his pocket. I asked, "What's that?"

He replied, "You tell me."

So I picked through the papers and saw that they were the numbers that I had gotten from guys while I was out at the club. I began to laugh because it was funny how all of a sudden, his insecurities had kicked in.

I never denied they were mine; I asked him, "What's your point?"

He then pulled out from underneath the couch cushion some sheets of paper. Turns out he had compared the numbers he found to the phone bill, and saw I had been calling. He had taken the time to highlight each one. I began to laugh even more. Sarcastically, he said, "It's funny?"

I replied, "Yes, because at least I didn't do anything with any of them. I was just talking, and that's all." I went to grab the paper from him.

He caught my arm and twisted hard, like he was ringing out a wet towel. I started to scream because he was hurting me. He got up and walked out. I couldn't move my wrist; I was in pain. I called my Uncle Matthew to take me to the emergency room at Kaiser. On the way there, he asked what had happened. I just said I fell while I was chasing our dog Peach through the apartment complex. My Uncle Matthew just looked at me like *Yeah right*. He knew I was lying.

The doctor diagnosed me with a fractured wrist, put me in a mini-cast, and sent me home. As we pulled up, I saw Ryan's car in the carport.

My uncle said, "I am not coming in because I don't want to say anything to Ryan."

Deep down inside, I was wishing he would get out of the car and tell him, "Hey man, it's not okay for you to be putting your hands on my niece!" or something to that effect. I just got out of the car and said, "Thanks for taking me."

As I walked to the doorstep, I saw Ryan wave to my uncle as he pulled off. When I got in the house, Ryan asked, "What happened to you?"

I screamed, "You did this!"

He replied, "I did that? Yeah right! You just want some attention."

I said, "Look, stupid, no one wants this kind of attention! What is wrong with you?"

He asked, "So what's for dinner?"

I said, "I know you don't expect for me to cook dinner now!"

"Yes," he replied.

Needless to say, he and I both went to bed hungry that night. This was unbelievable that he was that insensitive and abusive, and I was stuck in this crazy-ass relationship.

After him putting his hands on me for the second time, I was just distraught. I should have left him, but I could again hear my mom telling me that if I moved out with Ryan, I couldn't go back there. I began to despise him for what he was putting me through. I felt trapped, so I began to gradually act out which would eventually escalate to more serious repercussions.

One night, I guess you can say evilness got the best of me. He told me what club he was going to—the Golden Tail in LA. After he rolled out of the driveway, I decided I would take a drive down to the club too. Around 1:00 a.m., I got in the car. I arrived forty-five minutes later to find his car in the club parking lot. I knew driving down that I had no intentions of even going inside. However, I just felt mischievous. I used my spare key to his car to move his car to the other side of the parking lot at the club. Then I sat there, waiting for him to come out. Oh my goodness, to see the look on his face trying to find his car in the parking lot while wandering around half drunk! That in itself was well worth driving down to the club.

When he got home, he apologized for being late. He said that his cousin Myron was taking too long talking to a girl, and that is what took so long. I just looked at him with a smirk on my face and said, "Not a problem." He couldn't even tell the truth about that! He was such a liar even when he didn't have to be. Though moving his car was an amateur move, it was the start of more to come.

Ryan and I were still together for my twenty-first birthday. Anyone that knows me knows that I like to party it up big for my birthday. So I decided to throw a party for myself at the Golden Tail. I found a fly outfit. I scheduled a hair appointment and a nail appointment.

When my birthday came, I must say I was looking good and feeling good. A few hours before the party was to start, I was in LA, having my day of beauty treatment in preparation for my special event. While leaving the nail shop, I happened to be passing by Art's Wings & Things on Crenshaw when I saw Garin. I stopped and asked Garin if he was going to be in attendance at the party.

He told me, "You know that I do not do clubs!"

I said, "Come on, just for me, please? I'm the birthday girl."

He looked at me and said, "I will see what I can do."

I got back in the car with a hope in my heart that he would be in attendance at my party. I must say, I brought my twenty-first birthday in like a rock star. My closest friends and family were around and I was dancing the night away, looking good while doing it. I shut down the club that night. They had to turn on the lights and ask for us to leave.

Ryan, my best friend Taylor and I were the last to leave out. While walking to the parking lot, I spotted a navy-blue Toyota Land Cruiser parked in the parking lot. I said, "Naw, it couldn't be."

Taylor said, "What?"

"Doesn't that look like Garin's car?"

"Sure does," she agreed.

I said, "Someone is sitting in the car." I began to slowly approach the car, and to my surprise, it was Garin. I turned to Taylor. "Oh my God, it's Garin!"

Ryan was like, "Garin?!?!?"

I started to approach the Land Cruiser faster. As I got to the window on the passenger side, the window slowly rolled down, and I peeked my head in. Garin said, "Happy birthday, pretty girl."

Oh my God! I literally could have died right there in disbelief. This man had sat outside the club waiting for me to come out just to say happy birthday! That meant so much to me that words can't even explain it. Taylor approached the car too, since she already knew Garin, and she said a quick hello.

As I looked out of the corner of my eye, I could see Ryan coming towards the car. I quickly went over to him, gave him the keys to the car, and told him I would be there in a second. He looked like he wanted to grab me by my hair and drag me to the car. He did not have a choice except do as I requested. Taylor started walking to my car as I was heading back toward Garin's car.

I went over to the driver's side, and he told me, "You know I don't do clubs, but I wanted to make sure that I came to wish you a happy birthday."

I told him, "Thank you so much! I'll be talking to you soon!" He started the car as I walked away.

You could tell that Ryan was fuming. When we got to Taylor's house, I pretended like I had to run in to get something from her. When we got into her house, we giggled about how mad Ryan was. She jokingly stated, "Make sure you call me tomorrow so I can make sure you're alive, because he looked like he wanted to kill you!"

I hugged her goodbye and walked back to my car. That forty-five minute drive home was the longest ride ever. I was plagued, tormented with accusations about Garin. Ryan accused me of secretly still having a relationship with Garin, or that Garin was trying to steal me away from him. The truth was, Ryan was jealous of Garin and viewed him as a threat. In the end, Garin would be a threat to every new man that entered into my life.

Ryan – Gone Too Far

After my birthday party, I realized that Ryan was not going to change. Ryan began to realize that he wasn't going to change either. We loved each other to a certain extent, but we knew that things just couldn't work themselves out. He had done too much to forgive and too much to forget, and it was time to move on.

Ryan moved in with his stepbrother that lived probably about twenty minutes from us. Since he wasn't too far from me, it gave him room to still come by the house. The problem was that we had been together for some time, and it takes some time to get over someone. You have to remember though, when you're trying to get over someone, it's best that you stay away from them.

This wasn't the case for us. The first two weeks that Ryan was out of the house, he came by on certain days. On one particular day before he came by, I had just come from the family planning clinic. Once again, I was pregnant, and I didn't know what to do.

When he got to my house that day, I gave him the news about the pregnancy. He definitely wasn't excited, and the look on his face was of pure distress. I explained to him that I didn't want to have any children with him because he already had two other children, and that he and I were not together and were not getting back together. I let him know all he had to do was to transport me to the clinic to get the procedure done. He agreed. However, when the day came for me to go to the clinic, he was nowhere to be found. I waited and waited and still he never showed or called.

Once my appointment time had passed, I called my friends LaToya and Neena to come by and pick me up. When they arrived, I got in the car and I told them we were going on a drive-by. A drive-by to me was driving past someone's house to see what they were doing or who they were doing.

So we went by his stepbrother's house, but there was no sign of Ryan. Then we went past his cousin's house, and voila, there he was. He was outside playing a game of basketball with his cousin when he was supposed to be taking me to the clinic. Now I believe that when a man gets you pregnant that he should be the one to accompany you to get the procedure done. That's just the right thing to do. That's the least he could do.

So we waited around until it got a little dark outside. I got out of the car and went into his car with the spare key that I still had. I came upon a gallon-size Ziploc bag of weed. Ryan used to sell weed before we met. I can only assume that he went back to selling it once we stopped talking. I was so angry that the only thing I could think of at that moment was to take the weed. Don't get me wrong, I have never smoked pot my entire life, nor did I start on that day. After LaToya and Neena got back to the house, I flushed the baggy of weed down the toilet. See, the principle of it is not that I wanted the weed, but his ass was going to suffer a profit loss behind not keeping his word.

In the days that followed, I made his life a living hell, because he was acting as if I said I was going to keep the child. All I needed from him was to show up, take me to the clinic, and then drop me back off at home. Instead, that was too much to ask. I was just pissed off, and I wanted him to know how badly he was acting.

When we were together, he used to bump Tupac's "All Eyez On Me" because he used to think that he was so fine that all eyes were on him. Pleaaaaaaaaaasseeeeee!!! So I engraved "All eyes on me" on his driver's side door. He wanted all eyes on him? Well, now he had it. I'm sure whenever he was at a stoplight, all eyes were definitely on his door as people read what I had keyed.

Well, I couldn't stop there. The next day I went up to his job. Keep in mind that I still had the spare key to his car. So I opened up the door and I sprayed pepper spray throughout the car. I mostly hit areas that I knew that he would touch, like the steering wheel, gear shift, door locks, and window controls. I wasn't there to see his reaction once he got in that car, but I can only imagine. All I know is that pepper spray can cause difficulty with breathing, skin irritation, eye irritation, and maybe temporary blindness, and I hope he got all of the above.

I didn't want to overdo it, so I waited a couple of days to strike again. Before I could, he showed up at my doorstep. He was furious about me writing on his car. Of course I denied it. Who would tell the truth? Come on now! Deny, deny, deny… that is my defense. You only tell the truth if there's concrete proof. Otherwise, I didn't do it.

While he was standing there ranting and raving, I just stood there. After he was done, he walked toward his stepbrother's Tahoe truck. He turned around and said, "That's why I'm driving this." He drove away with a smirk on his face, but I knew that I would have the last laugh.

Instead of going to school that day, I went to his job instead. I found his stepbrother's car parked in the employee parking lot and keyed up the truck. I took that key from the front bumper to the back bumper and then I left. I know you may be thinking to yourself, "She's gone overboard", but you have to realize I was only hurting and lashing out while losing control all at the same time.

Three days later, he finally came to his senses. He said, "I'm sorry. I will take you to your appointment. I want to be there for you."

What a crock of bull! He just wanted the madness to end! I accepted his apology and I made the appointment to go get the procedure done. He was on time; we went and got it done.

On the way home, he stopped to get me something to eat. He came and sat inside with me for a little while, and then he said that he would be back later to check on me. That was around two o'clock. Later came, but it was damn near ten o'clock before I heard from his ass. I was more than upset at that point.

When he finally called, he said, "I'm not coming back over there."

I explained, "You still have my antibiotics in the car with you, and I need them back."

He said, "You'll be all right without them." Then I heard a click.

He had hung up on me! I was in total shock that this man had no sympathy for what I was going through, yet I still wasn't surprised, as this wasn't the first time a man showed his ass after taking me to the abortion clinic.

Even though my stomach was cramping and I was bleeding very heavily, I got dressed to drive over to his stepbrother's house to get my medication. When I arrived, I found Ryan walking a young lady from the house to her car.

At that very moment, I literally snapped. I got out of the car and I started screaming and yelling at the top of my lungs, "How could you? Why would you do this to me? I'm going to hurt you!"

The young lady looked astonished at what was going on. She hurried up, got in her car, and drove off. I then began swinging on him with my fists. I heard him saying, "You're crazy! You're crazy!"

The nerve of him! I had just gotten off the abortion table for him, and there he was romancing another woman, less than eight hours later. I was outdone. He ran in the house like a little punk and closed the door. I proceeded to get in my car and I took off. I ended up on the same road as the young lady that had just left his house. I became enraged when I saw her. At that very moment, the lights went off in my brain, and rage and insanity took over.

I got on the side of her and gestured for her to pull over the car. I have no clue why I wanted this girl to pull this car over. However, when she didn't comply with my request, I began to swerve in and out of my lane, trying to get her to pull over.

That didn't work; it only frightened her. She hopped an island with her truck, and I followed her. She was heading back in the direction of his house. I felt as if I had to stop her, so I took my car and rammed it into the back of hers.

I can honestly say, looking back at that point, I truly had lost my sanity for a moment – well, for more than one moment. I guess after hitting her car the second time, I finally came out of whatever trance I was in. I quickly came to a stop once I realized what I had done. But it was way too late. The only thing that I could do was go home and wait to see what the consequences for my actions would be. I honestly can identify with the show *Snapped*. People often wonder how people can lose control and end up in jail. Literally, your common sense and judgment departs and rage takes over. If a person is not able to snap back out of it, the consequences can be deadly.

Probably an hour later, the police department was at my door to arrest me for assault with a deadly weapon. They asked me to confirm my identity to ensure that they were picking up the right person. I showed them my ID. I was placed in handcuffs, read my rights, and placed in the back of a police car. I was transported to jail, where I was fingerprinted, photographed, and searched. I was then taken to a holding cell where I was alone for about six hours. I made multiple phone calls to my friends and family, hoping to get some peace of mind, some help, and some understanding to get through this mess that I had created for myself.

After six hours, I was placed in the general population with real inmates. I was given granny panties, a pair of white basketball tube socks, burgundy jelly shoes, and an orange jumpsuit. I spent about an hour with the general population before my name was finally called.

My mother had posted bail for me. My bail was $3,000, which was 10% of $30,000. I was placed in a room to get dressed in the clothes that I was arrested in the previous night. I was given back my personal property. I was escorted by a guard to a room that led out into a hallway, which in turn led to another door. When I finally opened it, there were many people waiting for their loved ones to get out of jail. There was one person missing: my mother.

I must say, my mother is a cold piece of work. She must have been disgusted with me on that day to post my bail and then leave me there. I called my Uncle Matthew, who lived about twenty minutes from where the jail was located. He and his wife Kathy came and picked me up. I should have walked home. Instead, I had to endure him busting my chops regarding my arrest. I felt like he was Dr. Phil. He just kept going on and on about how wrong my actions were. I'm sitting there like *Duh, doesn't he think I know that by now? I just spent the night in jail.* I wished there was a mute button so he could have just shut the hell up.

They dropped me off at my house. When I got in the house, I just felt so lonely and hurt. It felt like I had just hit rock bottom, and no one was around to help me get my life back in order. Sure enough, I had made my bed and I was definitely lying in it, but it still hurts all the same.

I let days go by without eating or drinking anything. It felt as if I was trying to will myself away from this earth. I know that Ryan and I had broken up, but it was just the way he had treated me all throughout our relationship that bothered me. Then for him to turn around and do this... I was the one who was hurting. I realized that I no longer needed him because he had turned his back on me in my deepest hour of need. I even entertained the thought of suicide.

One night, it got so bad that I called my mother at 1:00 a.m. She came over to sit with me for the night. I can recall her teasing me that Ryan must have really put some whip appeal on me for me to be in this shape. Comic relief was just what I needed to break up the nostalgia. She could be a cold piece of work, but she knew when to show tough love, and she knew when to give that true, motherly love...unconditional love. She helped me get through the night, and assured me that everything would be all right.

In my "woe is me" phase, I called on Garin. Garin would come and keep me company to help get through the night. He was always someone I could depend on. He had always shown how much love and compassion that he had for me.

Two weeks after the "snapped" situation, I received a letter in the mail stating that I needed to appear in court for assault with a deadly weapon for using my car to try to assault the young lady. The court date was to determine if I was guilty or innocent of the charges. I knew that I was guilty; however, after being in jail for almost twelve hours, I never wanted to go back. Jail is not a good place to be, no matter what length of time it may be.

So I discovered who the girl was, where she lived, and where she worked. I made a phone call to her. I apologized for my actions, but also let her know that if she showed up in court for me hitting the back of her car, that one incident would be the least of her problems. Needless to say, she didn't show up and all charges were dropped against me, since it was my first offense, and there were extenuating circumstances clouding my judgment. The court felt the need to still punish me by suspending my license. I was just glad that I wasn't going to jail...again! Ryan attempted to call me a few times after that escapade with him, but I washed my hands of him.

The temptation to get even presented itself one more time when the finance company for his car called my house and asked to speak with him. I told them he no longer resided at my residence. They asked if I knew where he lived or worked because he was behind on his car payment and they needed to pick up his car.

When they said that, it was like a light bulb went off in my head. Why not grab this moment of opportunity? I was more than cooperative in giving them the information about his new resident and employment.

Happy Kennedee, sad Ryan. His car was repo'ed the following day. How do I know that? The finance company called me back to thank me for helping them locate the vehicle. Go figure!

It wasn't until 2001 that I ran into Ryan at the mall while shopping. He looked the same, still had that cocky all-eyes-on-me attitude. He seemed happy to see me. He complimented me on how nice I looked. During the short time that he and I were together, we had gotten tattoos of one another's names. He lifted his sleeve to show me that he had my name covered with a panther. He then took his right index finger and tugged at my tank top. He smiled as he saw that his name was still on me. He gave me that "all eyes on me" smirk like he used to and I in turn gave him the evil eye.

He asked, "Why do you still have my name on you?"

All I could do was stand there and look stupid. He was correct; his crusty name was still on me. I couldn't stand to see the look on his face about this tattoo. I knew I had to remove it. Four years later, I found a place that was very reasonable and had it removed, and I was glad that I did. Though the tattoo was removable, unfortunately, the memories between him and I weren't. I have yet to run into him again, and to be honest, I hope I never do.

I guess I spoke too soon, because while writing this chapter about Ryan, he found me on the Internet through one of those social networking sites. He sent me a friend request. I wanted to press the ignore button, however, my curiosity got the best of me, and I pressed confirm. I guess I wanted to see what was going on with him, and I wanted him to know I was doing just fine without him.

When I clicked on his page, he had minimal pictures or information about himself posted. The few pictures that he had posted did not prove to be a good look. He had aged, and badly at that. He wrote on my wall, "It's good to see you. I left my information in your inbox. I'm not big on the web stuff, so maybe you can text me and we can hang sometime. Tell your family hello."

I think my blood pressure went up two notches after reading that. It's one thing to friend someone on these social networking sites, but rekindling an old flame is something that will never happen. How dare he think that I would want to hang out after everything that he had put me through? And for him to say tell my family hello? Are you serious? My mother would have choked me out for uttering this man's name. I didn't respond to the Wall post, but I did write him an e-mail. It read:

Ryan,
I didn't receive a message with your info, but I saw your Wall post. I don't think that contacting you off the website would be a good idea. It took a long time for me to get over everything that I went through with you. I was young and didn't know any better, but I have learned from my past, and I thank you for indirectly helping me become the person that I am now. I want you to know that I harbor no hard feelings toward you. I am glad to see you. I am glad to know that you are doing well. If you would like to keep in touch on the website that would be great, if not I can understand that too.
Peace & Blessings,

Kennedee

P.S. I finally got my tattoo removed :)

Ryan left my life in shambles. He not only left me emotionally hurt, but he also left me in a financial bind. When he and I decided to move in together, most of the bills and the apartment were in my name. When he left, I tried to maintain without him there. However, the financial struggle became too much. I ended up moving from the apartment, and my credit was charged for the remainder of the lease. For years, the results of this situation made it almost impossible for me to get a place in my name without providing a huge deposit. It took me years to get my credit back to where I didn't need a co-signer for anything. I harbor no ill feelings with Ryan, but it's hard to forget what he did to me. I can't forget what he did; however, I can forgive him, and that I can live with.

Jace – The Good Ones Always Leave Too Soon

You would think after such bad luck on Crenshaw that I would stay far away from there. I couldn't help myself though. Crenshaw used to be the spot. It was a place where you could meet a bonafide baller. Guys would be down there in Range Rovers, Mercedes-Benz's, BMW's, and Porsches. You name it, it was out there. I used to go down on Crenshaw very often, so I knew who the usuals were.

On Labor Day weekend of 1997, I found some fresh meat out there, and his name was Jace. My girls and I were rolling down Crenshaw when I spotted him in his black Range Rover on rims. We pulled up to the side of him, and I was like "Hey!"

He looked over, smiled, and said, "Pull over at the gas station."

We complied with his request. When he got out of the car, I must say, I was not impressed with his height. He was a little short for my taste. He was about 5'6" or maybe 5'6 ½". Either way, I was still taller than him.

There was something about his swagger that made me want to get to know him better anyway.

When he approached my window, you could tell that he wanted me to be impressed by his car, the Rolex on his wrist, and the cell phone in his hand. I would be frontin' if I said he didn't have my attention at that point. I mean, really, what woman wants a broke man? We exchanged numbers, and he called me later that night to see what I was doing. But I was busy, and he didn't like that.

I have to say, there was one thing about me. When I was in a relationship, I was loyal, but when I was single, I loved to mingle. Most guys didn't like me to mingle, so they would immediately make me their girlfriend.

The next day, Jace called again. He asked, "May I take you out today?"

I said, "I had already made plans with my girls."

"Bring your girls with you. I have some friends for them."

I agreed to go. He picked me and my girls up with his boys in tow. We ended up at the movies. He wanted to see *Air Force One*. Sometimes it is better to go on dates by yourself, because one of my girlfriends decided that she didn't want to see the movie and threw a tantrum. At this point, I was becoming more impressed with him, because instead of him allowing her to ruin our date, he purchased a different ticket to the movie she wanted to see. Our first date, I must say, was good.

The more I got to know him, the more impressed I became with him. He was distinguished and accomplished. He had a degree, his own business, his own house, and most of all, his own money. We went out on many dates, and I enjoyed his company very much.

At the time, I was not living near Los Angeles. I was about forty-five minutes away. He wanted me to be closer to him, so I started making plans to move closer. That way, we would be able to spend more time together.

One night, we went out to the Cheesecake Factory in the Marina and had dinner. We discussed me moving to LA and having a stronger relationship with one another. That night went so well that I was sad to see it come to an end. I remember us pulling up to my house and kissing him goodbye. I got out of the truck and opened the back seat door to get my doggie bag.

He turned around and stated, "I would like to take you home with me tonight, but I'm tired and I have to get up for work early in the morning."

I replied," Don't worry about it. I'll see you sometime this weekend." I blew him a kiss, closed the car door, and he watched from the car as I walked to my front door.

Two days later while I was working, I received a phone call from a friend informing me that Jace had been shot and killed by two men at his home the previous night. All I could do was sit there in disbelief that a man who I was with less than 48 hours ago was now dead. I began to think about what could have been with us and the times that we shared, and I started to cry. It's funny how you can see someone one day and they can be gone the next. Never did I imagine that something like that would happen to him. He was shot in the garage of his home in Baldwin Hills. According to some neighbors, they saw two black men leaving the scene on foot. They robbed him of his wallet and Rolex watch, and then shot him point blank in the chest. By the time the police had arrived, he was already dead.

I contemplated for days whether or not I should attend his funeral. I just don't do well with funerals; they just seem to exhaust me emotionally. I really didn't want to attend by myself, because I had only met two of his friends, and I wouldn't know anyone else. My homegirl Carla and my homeboy Jacari ended up attending the funeral with me.

The service was held at a very large church in Los Angeles. The church was huge; it was beyond its capacity. The church was filled with all races: Blacks, Asians, Hispanics, and Caucasians. The service was a tear jerker. They opened the floor to have people come up and say two minutes of acknowledgement about Jace. I would say about 20-30 people got up. There was nothing but good words spoken about this man; he had definitely touched many lives. This was the longest funeral I had ever attended. It lasted three and a half hours.

When it came time for the viewing of his body, I battled within to get the courage to see Jace one last time. When it was our row's turn, Jacari helped me up and Carla was right behind me. As I approached the casket, I could feel my knees getting weak. Just when my knees were about to buckle, Jacari was right there to catch me. Jacari held me tight and closely by the shoulders while Carla stood behind with her hand on my back.

To see him just lying there…it was overwhelming. I could hear loud sounds of weeping. I recognized that sound. It was me, crying uncontrollably. I was saddened to see a life taken away too soon. I cried so much that I begin to hyperventilate. The attendants from the mortuary came, took me from Jacari, sat me down in a chair, handed me a glass of water, and began to rub my back to calm me down. After I got control of my emotions, Jacari and Carla took me to the car. Jacari ended up driving me to the cemetery for the last of the services. The only things that come too soon in life are death and sorrow.

Jace was only thirty-two, and he was murdered for reasons that only the killers know. The police never arrested anyone nor had any suspects behind what happened that fatal night. I visit his mausoleum at least once a year. I never want to forget the man who gave me the first glimpse of how a lady should truly be treated. I get teary-eyed just thinking of the possibilities, of what could have been with him. He may be gone, but he definitely hasn't been forgotten.

Jackson – Too Fine To Be True

It was a few weeks after Jace's funeral when I was at my cousin's house visiting. I walked into his room to find him and his friends hanging out. Most of my cousin's friends were very handsome, but they were very young. When I walked into the room, I really didn't take notice of anyone in particular because they were not in my age bracket. I was hanging out in the living room when one of the guys came out to sit at the dining room table. I really didn't pay any attention at first until he said hi. I looked over to see who was speaking to me.

He was a light caramel color with nice features, and he was tall, just how I like them. He asked me my name and I replied, "Kennedee. What's your name?"

"Jackson."

"How old are you?"

"I'm twenty-two years old."

I said, "You're hanging out with my fourteen year old cousin and you're twenty-two? I think I'm going to need to see some ID."

He pulled out his ID, and sure enough, he was twenty-two years old. Boy oh boy was I glad! We exchanged numbers, and he called. When we talked over the phone, I soon realized he was definitely not a phone person, because our phone conversations were very brief. Typically, when you begin to date someone, you spend hours on the phone getting to know one another.

We made plans to go to breakfast. He picked me up, and we drove to the restaurant. Unlike previous guys that I had dated, he seemed a little quiet, but that didn't bother me because he was fine. During the meal, we just went over the basics, since I wasn't able to obtain all this information over the phone. I wanted to know what he liked to do for fun, where he worked, how many kids he had, etc. Looking back, I can see that we probably didn't have that much in common, but the physical connection was off the chain. I mean, he did look like he would be a good lover. So against my better judgment, I went ahead and proceeded with a relationship with him.

Jackson had a child already, but by this time, men without children were becoming very scarce. Before I continue with my story about Jackson, I must tell you that our relationship never started off physical. We actually dated one another first, but somehow, it ended up physical. I eventually moved back to LA, and thereafter, it was on every night between Jackson and me.

Though we were both young and I had been with older men, Jackson was very experienced. When we had sex, it was amazing, it was like pure lust. It was just that hot, nasty, sweaty, passionate sex. It was the kind of sex you would be thinking about at work and could not wait to get home to do it all over again. I was really digging him. I liked his style, I liked the sex, and he was fine. I know I already mentioned he was fine, but damn it, he was. He looked like an off-brand Ginuwine.

Jackson was fine...so fine that he knew it too, and that was his problem. See, the problem with fine guys is that they already know, and so when they get tired of messing around with you, they can always find someone new. One day, I was in the car with my girl Yuri. We just happened to turn down the wrong street, and lo and behold, we see Jackson getting into his car with some girl. I told Yuri turn this car around so I can see what the hell is going on. By the time we turned around, he was already pulling off. I told her to follow him, and she did.

Jackson started weaving in and out of lanes and going through the streets so quickly that we could hardly keep up with him. When he finally saw that we were going to continue to follow him, he pulled over and got out of the car. He explained by saying that he was with his baby mama and that his son was in the car with him. He said that we needed to stop following him because his baby mama would trip out on him.

I asked, "What the hell are you doing with her anyways?"

He replied, "I just took her and the baby to the doctor."

I said, "If there is nothing going on, how come she can't get out the car and you introduce me to her?"

"That's not going to happen." He turned to Yuri and said, "If you continue to follow me, I will hit your car."

Yuri with her scary self said, "Maybe we should just go home."

So she dropped me off at my house. I jumped on the phone and I paged him. Now how crazy is that? I just found him with someone else, yet I still wanted to see him. It must've been the sex - ha ha! He returned my page within less than a minute.

I told him, "You have some explaining to do."

"I'll be right over." He only lived right around the corner from me.

As soon as I opened the door, he came in apologizing, and we made up. And by making up, I mean making up. I should have never called him over that day after I caught him in that lie. But it was too late; I was already sprung. Me being dick whipped would be the cause of my blindness.

It wouldn't be long again before my foot would be back on his neck again for lying. Jackson and I had plans to go the movies. I had been anticipating this date all week, but he called the night before to say that he was going to San Diego instead. He said that he would be attending the Chargers football game. I have never been a fan of football, but I had the sense to ask my homeboy Jacari if the Chargers were playing the next day. His answer was no. Words cannot express how disappointed I was to find out that Jackson was lying to me.

By the 90's, Caller ID had come into play, and everybody and their mama had it, including Jackson. When Saturday came, I wanted to call and see if he would answer. However, if he saw my number, I knew he wouldn't answer. So I had my homegirl Taylor call him on three-way. The phone rang, and when the person on the other line answered, it was Jackson.

I quickly said, "Jackson, I thought you were going out of town!"

He said, "Who is this?"

"Kennedee."

"This isn't Jackson."

I said, "Well, who this is?"

He said, "This is his brother, Ray."

I frowned. "Oh, really? You guys really sound the same."

"Yeah, people tell us that all the time."

"Can you please tell him I called?"

Before we could hang up, the phone was being snatched from his "brother". There was a female on the other line saying, "Bitch, don't be calling Jackson! Who the fuck is this?"

I fumed, "This is his girlfriend! Who the hell is this?"

"Girlfriend?"

"Yes, that's what I said!" I retorted.

I heard the phone hang up. I called back, but someone kept hanging up. So I hung up and went to go get in my car, because Jackson only lived less than five minutes away.

When I arrived at his house, there he was coming out of the house with another female. I was infuriated as I watched him cross the street and get in the car with her. As they drove off, I ducked down, hoping that he wouldn't notice me or my car. I felt so betrayed by him that he could sit there and lie like that. You would think I would have become immune to bullshit like this, but it would be like a trigger would come on, and I couldn't turn it off. All I could see was red, which was anger, and anger had become revenge (at least in my mind).

I hadn't come prepared to do any harm or damage, so I immediately started to look around. My eyes came across a huge decorative rock in one of his neighbor's yard. I hurriedly ran across the street, got the rock, and jumped back into my car. I drove up the street and parked right across from his house. I got out of the car, began to run to towards his car, and threw the rock through his back window. I didn't look back as I heard the sound of glass breaking. I was too busy trying to get out of there before I got caught.

I went straight home. Just in case he called, I could at least act like I had been sitting there all night long. Not to my amazement, he did call and asked if I had busted out the front window of his car.

I thought I busted out his back window? I had become too slick to fall for *trick* words. I softly said, "No, I didn't bust out any window in your car. Why would I do something like that? Ooh! Wait! I thought you were supposed to be in San Diego?"

He angrily responded, "I came back early." There he was, still lying…

I began to tell him how bad I felt that someone would do something like that. All the while, I sat there laughing inside, because I knew it was me.

He said, "I have to go, I don't feel like talking."

Yeah, I'm sure he didn't. I just could not wrap my head around his logic of why he came over my house the next day to visit me, even though I was the one he suspected of damaging his car. Looking back, I should have been completely done with him, because I saw what his capabilities were. He was a liar and a cheater. There was just something about Jackson that made me gravitate to him. That evening he stopped by my house I walked him out to his car. As I saw his back window covered with cardboard and duct tape a small part of me felt bad for doing what I did especially after the pitiful look on his face as he walked to his car. Even after all that, we continued to see each other for two years on and off.

Things were working out between us and seemed to be going very well, until one morning while I was dropping off my cousin Derwin at school. I spotted Jackson dropping off some young girl. I saw him tonguing her down with my own eyes. This time, he couldn't use the excuse of "It's my baby mama, my cousin, my homegirl" or whatever he thought of at the moment.

As the young girl got out of the car, he watched, looking like a salivating dog. I was disgusted and mortified, not only because he was cheating, but because he was pulling an R. Kelly move. I honked the horn and waved so that he would know that I saw him.

I called him later on that evening. This incident had happened right after Christmas, so, I told him that he needed to bring back the Nintendo that I bought for him Christmas. I said, "Bring it tonight, or else!"

He yelled, "Or else what!"

I screamed, "Or else you going to have to replace another back window!" I only said that because I knew he knew all along that I was responsible for that night.

Later on that night, my doorbell rang. I opened up the door to find a bag with the Nintendo inside. Granted, I didn't want the Nintendo for myself, but he for damn sure wasn't keeping it either! I ended up giving it to my cousin Kelvin; I knew he would appreciate it more than Jackson did. I was done with Jackson—at least, that's what I thought.

Crazy thing is, it never ended there. He and I continued to date from our early 20's to our early 30's, eleven years of dating on and off. So unfortunately, this will not be the last of Jackson in this book. On to the next one.

<u>Desmond – A Taste of Crazy</u>

I met a guy while coming out of my job. He caught my attention because his clothes were well put together. I went up to him and said, "You look really nice."

He smiled and said, "Thank you." I smiled back and turned to walk away. He called out, "What's your name?"

"Kennedee," I replied as I made my way back to him.

He said, "I'm Desmond. Do you think that I could take you out sometime?"

"Sure!"

We exchanged numbers. He called me later that night and asked to take me to lunch the next day. I told him, "I can't, my girl Neena is coming over and we're going to this sale at Macy's."

He said, "How about I take you and your friend to lunch?"

I told him, "That might be okay, but I still need to go to the mall."

"No worries. After lunch, we'll go together and I'll buy you whatever you want."

Ding, ding, ding...we have a winner!!! He was in there with that statement. It's always better to spend someone else's money than your own. Since he offered...well...how could I refuse?

The next day Neena and I met Desmond at Macy's. I met him with a hug and slight kiss on the cheek. I introduced him to Neena; they shook hands and spoke to one another. We then walked into Macy's.

Neena and I immediately went to the shoe department. We tried on shoes trying to pick our favorites. Desmond just sat there with a smile on his face. We finally decided on which shoes we wanted about an hour later. He walked the pairs up to the counter, the cashier rang my items up, and Desmond pulled out his wallet and just paid. I turned to Neena and saw that she had only picked two pairs of the several shoes that we tried on.

I asked, "Why don't you have any of the others?"

She said, "I didn't think I have enough."

Desmond told Neena to go get the other shoes that she wanted. She found the store clerk, and she went and got the shoes she had put back. Desmond paid for her shoes too. I was impressed. She and I both walked out of Macy's with our hands full and a smile on our faces.

We had spent a little too much time in Macy's. We ran out of time to have lunch with him. He said he had somewhere else to be. I kinda felt bad for not having lunch with him after he had spent his money on the both of us. I told him, "Well, since you have been so nice, how about you let us cook you dinner tonight at your place?"

He agreed, "Cool." He handed me fifty bucks to get whatever I needed from the store. He gave me his address and said to meet him at 6:00 p.m. Neena and I headed back to my house, and we gloated about our new shoes, which didn't cost a dime out of our pockets.

An hour before we were supposed to arrive at his house, we made our way to the store. We used the fifty dollars to buy shrimp for shrimp scampi, fresh vegetables, and potatoes for the dinner. We got strawberries, pound cake, and whipped cream for the dessert. Neena always complimented me on how well I cooked. She commented, "Girl, cooking all this, he ain't going to never want you to leave!"

I thought, *That's the idea.* Who knew her words would ring true later on that evening?

We left the store and headed to his house. We arrived on time and I had dinner ready within forty-five minutes. Neena, Desmond, and I sat in his living room area enjoying the delicious meal I cooked while watching TV and having small talk. When we were finished eating everything, Neena washed the dishes as Desmond and I continued to talk. The more we talked, the more I felt like that this might not work. There was just something off about him. I couldn't put my finger on it, but something wasn't right. After Neena was done, I told Desmond that we had to go.

He became upset. "Why y'all leaving? It's still early."

I said, "We already made previous plans and we have to go."

He asked, "Why didn't you tell me that earlier?"

"Because I didn't know I had to!"

He whined, "So you guys can't stay a little while longer?"

I said, "No, we have to go. Either you can walk us out or we can find our way out ourselves."

He got up and walked us outside to the car. He came to the car door window, and he said, "Kennedee, are you sure you guys can't stay?"

"I'm sure."

"Well, just call me later."

I said I would. Truth be told, we didn't have anywhere to be, but once again, there was something about him that wasn't right. The way he was so persistent about us staying longer totally added to my doubt. On the way home, I explained to Neena why I wanted to leave. She said she got the same vibe. She also said that she felt as if he thought we both was going to get with him, like maybe he wanted a threesome or something, and when he saw we were about to bounce, he got upset.

Neena was spending the weekend at my house, so we were just chilling. I got a phone call around 10:30 p.m. from my Aunt Tia, letting me know my Aunt Bethany had just passed away. I was speaking with her about the when, how, and where when my line beeped. I clicked over, and it was Desmond.

He said, "I thought I asked you to call me?"

"I was going to, but I'm on the other line right now. My aunt just passed away."

"Well call me back."

"Okay." I clicked over and finished the conversation with my aunt. I hung up with her and I explained to Neena what had just happened.

I fell asleep and forgot to call Desmond back. The next morning, which was a Saturday, we were awakened at 7:30 a.m. by the phone ringing. Neena answered it, and it was Desmond. Neena told him I was sleeping and she would have me call when I got up.

I asked, "Who was that... Desmond?"

She said, "Yeah."

When I finally did get my day started, I called him back. I told him I didn't think that things were going to work out between us. I offered to either return Neena's shoes and mine to him so he could get his money back, or we would just keep the shoes and I would just give the money directly to him so he wouldn't have to go back to the mall. He stated that he had enjoyed our company and he wasn't tripping so we could keep the shoes, and he understood. I said cool, and we hung up.

I had invited my homeboy Mace from work over to take a swim in the pool. I told him to bring a friend because I had my homegirl Neena over. He came through around 1:00 p.m. He didn't disappoint. He brought a nice-looking yellow boy with curly hair by the name of Derek. He and Neena hit it off quickly. We were having a good time at the pool, just kicking it, and talking.

Mace said, "What's up with some food?"

"How about I order a pizza?" I suggested.

Everyone agreed that would be cool. Neena and I went in the house, and when I went in my room to check my pager, I saw that I had ten pages on it. I went through the numbers. One of them was Desmond's number, and the other nine were the same number. I picked up the phone to call the number I didn't know, but I heard a stuttering dial tone, which meant I had a voicemail on the message center. I called the message center first. The message I retrieved was Desmond calling Neena and I bitches, and him saying that he wanted his shoes back.

He also said that if we didn't give them back, he was going to kill us.

I handed Neena the phone and replayed the message so she could hear it. She said, "You offered to give him back the shoes already. What is wrong with this fool? I told you something was off about him."

I called back the number from the pager. The person on the other end answered with, "Angelus Funeral Home, how may I help you?" I hung up.

Neena asked, "Who was that?"

"I think I had the wrong number. Can you hand me my pager so I can make sure I dialed the right number?" I called the number back again.

Again, someone answered, "Angelus Funeral Home, how may I help you?"

I said, "I'm sorry, I think I may have the wrong number," and then I hung up.

Neena asked again, "So who is it?"

"I think he paged me and put in the Angelus Funeral Home number."

"Oh, Lord!!!"

By that time, Mace and Derek were ringing the doorbell. Neena opened the door.

Mace asked, "What's taking you all so long?"

I came out of the bedroom and began to explain what had just happened. I sat down and just began to think about how I got myself into this mess. Everyone could see the distressed look on my face.

Neena came and sat down next to me. She said, "How do you want to handle this?"

I replied, "I'm going to call him and talk to him." Everyone had this strange look on their face when I said that. I picked up the phone and began to dial his number.

I guess he had caller ID, because when he answered, he said, "What do you want, bitch?"

I said, "I got your message, and I wanted to know, what's your problem?"

"I get tired of cute bitches like you thinking you can take advantage of people," he fired back.

"I wasn't trying to take advantage of you! When I saw that we weren't compatible, I offered to return the shoes, but you said to keep them. Now you want them back? I don't think so!"

He said, "If you don't give me back those shoes, I'm going to be waiting for you at your job."

"I ain't giving you shit back!" I told him before I hung up. This man was tripping thinking he was going to punk me! I turned to Neena. "Get the shoes he bought for us out of my room."

She looked at me, puzzled. "I thought you weren't giving them back?"

I said, "Just go get the shoes."

Neena brought the shoes into the living room. I began to take the shoes out of each shoebox. I then went onto the patio and came back in with a bag of charcoal. Neena asked, "What are you going to do with that? I thought we were ordering pizza."

I said, "Forget the pizza! He wants these shoes, he can have them! We are going over there and dropping them off!"

Everyone changed out of their swimwear. Neena got in the car with me. Mace and his friend got in his car and followed me over to Desmond's house.

Mace and I parked our cars about three houses up from Desmond's. I got out of the car and began to walk towards his house with two bags in my hand. I placed the bags on the porch, rang the doorbell, and took off running.

You might be thinking, "I thought she wasn't no punk?" I'm not, but you would run too if you had replaced the shoes in the shoeboxes with charcoal briquettes. That's what I was doing with that bag of charcoal. I already had offered this punk these shoes back, and initially he said no. Now he tries to call back and act a fool over it? Please! I wish I would! Pride can be one's downfall.

I ran to the car and jumped in. Mace pulled up on the side of my car. He asked, "Is everything okay?"

I replied, "Yeah."

Neena asked, "Did he open the boxes?"

"I don't know, I just put the boxes on the porch, rang the bell, and took off." Keep in mind that we are still sitting in our cars having this conversation on Desmond's street.

All of sudden I hear a car coming up the street. I looked in the rearview mirror, and it was Desmond. He was approaching us too fast on a residential street. I told Mace, "We gotta get out of here, here he comes!"

We started our cars, but before we could take off, he pulled up to the side of Mace's car and threw the two bags out the window. Out flew the boxes and black charcoal briquettes. Mace and I both floored our gas pedals.

I know my way around the Los Angeles area. However, we were in Baldwin Hills with all those Don Felipe, Don Jose, Don Juan, Don everything all over the place. I got turned around very quickly. I was in the front, Mace was in back of me, and Desmond was in back of Mace. I was really trying to obey traffic laws and keep everyone safe, but on a high-speed chase, this is not quite possible.

I stopped at a stop sign. Mace stopped too. I went, but Mace stayed. I was looking through my rearview mirror and I saw Mace start swerving from side to side. I saw him waving his hand out the window for me to just go. Mace had created a distraction that allowed me to get away from Desmond.

I began to drive aimlessly in this maze, trying to find my way to a main street. Finally, I hit La Brea. I pulled over at a gas station to use a pay phone to call 911. I explained to the operator what had happened. She said she was sending an officer to our location and that I should just wait. We were there for about fifty minutes.

While we were there, I got several pages that let me know someone had left me a voicemail. When I called back to see who it was, it was Desmond's voice.

The message said, "I'm going to kill you and your girl. I'm going to chop off your heads and send them to your parents. I'm going to find out where you both live and kill you in your sleep!"

I didn't even listen to the rest; I just hung up the phone. I explained to Neena what the voicemail had said. I told her I thought that we should leave the gas station and just go down to the police station instead of waiting. She agreed. We jumped in the car, went down to the police station, and explained the whole story to the desk sergeant. They filed a police report. They said they would be visiting his resident to speak with him, and they advised me to file a restraining order.

Neena and I went back to my house. I called Mace to see if he and his friend were ok.

He explained, "Desmond continued to follow me all the way into the 'hood. Once we got in the 'hood, Desmond finally turned around. Are you okay?"

I said, "Not really. I'm a little scared." To be honest, I was a whole lot scared. This man had really scared the crap out of me. This was my first time being in a situation like this, and I have to admit, the shoe didn't feel too good being on the other foot.

Mace asked, "Do you want me to come over?"

I quickly answered, "Yes!"

Mace and his friend came over and kept Neena and I company. We all joked about what had happened earlier that day. To be truthful, I think I was laughing to keep from crying, as I had really gotten myself into a bad predicament. I could see if I had spent some real time with this dude, or sexed him up. Maybe then he would have a right to be obsessed with me. But this man didn't even know me.

When it was time to go to bed, we all slept in the living room on the floor. I didn't get much sleep that night because I was afraid that Desmond somehow, some way, was going to find out where I lived and come in and kill all four of us. Every noise I heard literally had me on edge all throughout the night. This man had me more scared and paranoid than when Royce had threatened to kill me.

Come Monday morning, I walked into work, and my supervisor called me into the office. He told me that an unidentified caller had called to get my work schedule for the week. He explained to the caller that he was unable to give that information out and that the person had hung up the phone.

I couldn't believe this crazo had called my job trying to get my work schedule! I explained to my supervisor what happened during the weekend. My supervisor guaranteed that I would be safe at work. He asked for a description of Desmond, and he gave it to the security officers at the front door. I was also escorted to the parking lot for nearly a month behind this whole scenario.

I never saw or heard from Desmond again. I was scared for a while though. All this behind some shoes! I had enough money to buy my own shoes, however, I thought that using someone else's money was more beneficial to me. Consequently, something so innocent turned into drama-filled nonsense. You would think after getting a taste of craziness like this, I would have slowed down my crazy antics, but I just viewed it as luck. Once my terror of someone being crazy over me was over, I was back to living by my motto: you hurt me, and I am definitely going to give you something to think about as well as cry about!

Mace was a big help during the time I was harassed by Desmond. He would pick me up for work and drop me back off at home. Mace was a cutie, and a cool guy, but he was just young. I think he was like four years younger than me. He had the prettiest skin I have ever seen on a guy. He was a dark chocolate, and his skin was so smooth. He was about 6' tall and slim. He had the mannerisms of an old soul. He was just really cool, and that's how I ended up dating him. He would bring me lunch, and on our off days, we would go to the movies, out to dinner, bowling, just anything fun. The only thing that I didn't like about him was that he still liked hanging out with a bunch of his friends, but that's typical of youngsters.

One weekend, we made plans to go to Magic Mountain because our credit union was offering discounted tickets. The plan was that Mace was going to give me the money to purchase the tickets, and I would go pick them up. We had agreed that I would come by and pick up the money from his house on Thursday morning. He wasn't going to work because we had been in a car accident a few weeks prior, and he was going to physical therapy. We had totaled his car and his face had hit the windshield. He had a few bruises and cuts from the accident, and his shoulder was hurt as well, but he still felt like he was up to going to Magic Mountain. So I went to his house to pick up the money.

When I knocked on the door, I could hear him inside scrambling for something, then I heard, "Shhh!"

I was thinking to myself, *Here we go again - men and their cheating ways!*

When he opened the door all he had on were his pajama bottoms. He said, "What's up, why are you over here so early?"

"Remember, you are supposed to be giving me the money so that I can go and get the tickets for this weekend?" I reminded him.

"Come back later," he said as he attempted to close the door.

"Why later? I'm here now."

That's when I heard the voice of a young lady say, "Because I'm here right now."

I looked at him and said, "How could you?"

"How could I what?"

"Have some girl here when you and I are supposed to be together!" I fumed.

"Shut the hell up!" he yelled, then he slapped me.

I was so astonished that this man had just slapped me for no apparent reason. I looked at him and said, "You are going to be sorry that you did that!"

He smirked. "I bet!"

I started walking off his porch but then turned around and said, "You will see...you will see soon."

I went ahead and went to work. I was upset the whole day. I couldn't believe that his black self had put his hands on me. During my lunch break, I called my girl Neena and my cousin Derwin to tell them what had happened and to ask them to meet me at the house at 5:30 p.m.

When I got home from work, Neena, Derwin, and my cousin's friend Larry were waiting for me. I quickly ran into the house and threw on some sweatpants and some tennis shoes. We all hopped in Neena's car and drove over to Mace's house. When we arrived, Mace was on the porch with his homeboys, just kicking it. We all got out of the car and approached him.

Mace said, "What's this all about?"

I replied, "Did you really think that I was going to let you get away with slapping me? You must be out your mind!"

"You must be out *your* mind to think that I am about to let you and your folks try anything on my porch!" he shot back. He turned to his homeboy. "Go to the house and get the heat." His homeboy started walking past me and out the gate.

For some strange reason, those words didn't faze me. I walked towards Derwin, Larry, and Neena, who were still waiting outside the fence, and told them to go get into the car.

Neena asked, "What are you about to do?"

I said, "All you need to do is start the car and pull the car so the passenger side is facing his fence."

"Okay," she agreed reluctantly with a worried look on her face.

I walked back inside his fence and walked on his porch. "Now where were we?" I demanded.

He said, "You tell me!"

"I will tell you! What I want you to know is that it is never ever okay to put your hands on a woman, and I am going to make you remember that!"

"How you think you are going to do that?" he asked.

Before "that" could fully leave his lips, I was already coming out of my pocket with a can of real mace. I sprayed him right in the face, and I took off running. I could hear him yelling, "My eyes, my eyes!" as I dashed to the car.

I told Neena, "Hit it!" Neena took off speeding down the street.

"Oh my God, Kennedee, I can't believe that you did that!" my cousin said.

I shook my head. "Me either!"

Neena said, "I could hear him saying 'my eyes'!"

We all started laughing. I said, "I'm sure his eyes aren't the only thing that's burning, since he had cuts on his face from the car accident."

"Ooh!" everyone said in unison, then they started laughing hysterically.

The next day at work, everyone knew what had happened between Mace and me. He had come up there and told everyone before I could make it to work. The secret was out that Mace and I were an item and had an awful break-up. Mace was still out on medical leave, however, there was a pending investigation for him stealing from work. They found him on the security camera stealing corporate items. He ended up getting fired before getting off his medical leave. What a relief, because I could not bear to work with him after that incident. Just imagine how uncomfortable the work environment would have been after something like that happened! I was glad he was gone, because I didn't want to deal with drama at work.

One thing that I did learn from that situation was that you should never ever get romantically involved with someone from the workplace. When things go sour, it just makes for disaster. I would have given Mace a pass even though I caught him with another girl, but the moment he slapped me, it was lights out for him. I had not done anything to provoke him; he did it just because he thought he could. I think after that situation with Desmond, he must have thought I was some kind of chump.

Looking back at this situation, I am glad that the outcome wasn't worse than what it was. He actually sent his homeboy to go get a gun. That situation could have turned extremely bad very quickly. I am glad that I can look back and laugh with Neena and Derwin every time we talk about old times. They always say, "Remember that time you maced Mace?" and then we all started busting up laughing. With two back-to-back crazy incidents like that happening, I began to wonder if it was just me, or if it was the men I was attracting.

Nasir – Knight in Shining Platinum

B y this time it was 2000. I had relocated back to the Inland Empire from Los Angeles. It had been almost four years that I had been without my driver's license, since I had lost back in '96 behind that incident with Ryan and that girl. I also had been one year without a vehicle. Since I wasn't supposed to be driving, I sold it to lose the temptation of driving without a license. I decided it was time that I made some arrangements to get it back. I had to obtain an SSR-22 in order to get my license back. I went down to the DMV, showed my proof, took a test, and I had my new license. Not having a license for so long really made me value it even more once I got it again.

As soon as I got my license reinstated, I got a rental from Enterprise for the weekend, and I was on my way to LA. I went bowling with my homegirls Erin and Taylor and my homeboy Jacari. After we were done, we went to Denny's for some late-night grub. We were sitting there eating, laughing, and having a good time. The bill came and we paid it.

As we all walked out the door, I noticed a handsome young man approaching the door. He looked like a little baller type. He had on a Coogi sweater, some Sean John jeans, powder-blue Timberlands that matched the pattern in his sweater, and a platinum chain around his neck with diamond cuts. Our eyes immediately locked. He was about 5'6". He rocked a fade with a hint of waves, and he had a honey-brown complexion. He reminded me of the R & B singer Tank.

I really don't like short guys. They really have to have some type of swagger to them in order to catch my attention. But he certainly did that. He was on the phone while opening up the door to the entrance, so I went ahead and asked, "How are you doing?"

He looked at me strangely. "Are you talking to me?" A New York accent left his mouth as he spoke.

I said, "Yes, I'm talking to you! How are you doing?"

He told the person on the phone, "Let me call you back," and he hung up with them. He said, "I'm doing fine. How are you tonight?"

"I'm doing just fine," I told him.

"Are you going into the restaurant?"

"Well, we just finished eating and are on our way to another spot." As I was talking, Taylor and Jacari said goodnight and got in their cars and left. Erin was still at the entrance with me while I was speaking with him.

He asked me, "What's your name?"

"Kennedee; what's yours?"

"Nasir. Are you heading home?"

I said, "No."

"Would you like to do something with me?"

I asked him, "Like what?"

"What's open late around here?"

I laughed. "This is LA; nothing stays open too late. I tell you what, you can follow me to the Hollywood Park Casino."

He got in his car and Erin and I got into my car and went to the casino. Once he arrived, he seemed to be impressed with it from the outside. He said, "I have never been here. This seems like a cool spot."

I was thinking, *Yeah, it's all right cuz it's the only thing open.*

All three of us walked in the door to the bar area and sat down. After one drink, Erin decided to go find herself some male company. Nasir and I sat at the bar for three hours, just sitting there and talking. He told me that he was from New York and that he was a producer. I thought, *Here we go again with this.* He said he was thirty years old, and had a one-year-old daughter. His conversation was really cool. He didn't ask too much about my personal business, but he asked just enough questions to keep my attention. I liked that.

Finally, I looked at my watch and I said, "Oh my goodness, it's almost 4 o'clock in the morning! We should be going."

He said, "Before we go, I'd like to exchange numbers with you and give you a call the next time I'm out this way."

I asked, "How long will it be before you come down here again?"

He replied, "I normally come to LA every two weeks or at least once a month."

I explained, "The car that I have is a rental and I'm not sure when I'm getting a car of my own. I don't know if I will be able to see you once you come back down."

He said, "How much does it cost to rent a car for the weekend?"

I told him, "Probably around $100, but that's only if my grandfather will put it on his credit card again for me."

He went into his pocket, pulled out his wallet, reached in, and handed me a $100 bill. He told me to put the hundred dollar bill under my pillow and when he came back, he wanted me to rent a car to come see him. I was grinning from ear to ear. I was surely impressed at that moment that a man that had just met me less than three hours ago was now giving me money to hold onto to make sure I could see him again. I loved it.

It was a Friday night when I met him. By Sunday afternoon, he was ringing my phone. We talked for hours about everything, it seemed like. He said, "I'll be back down soon. Do you still have the money?"

I could not lie. "I spent the money already," I confessed.

He chuckled. "I figured you would. No worries. Give me your information, and I'll send you a Western Union."

I said, "Really?"

"Of course! Why wouldn't I? I said I wanted to see you. I will give you a call on Thursday to give you the information, and then I'll be down."

Man, I was impressed even more at this point. Thursday came, and he called to say that he had just sent me a Western Union for $300. I thought, *That is more than enough money to get the rental!* His plane was set to land around 10:00 p.m., so after work, I went to go get my hair and nails done and to pick up the rental that I had gotten that morning.

I met him at the Los Angeles Marriott near LAX. He was so happy to see me that he picked me up off the ground and hugged and kissed me. It had been so long since someone had shown me this type of affection that I have to say he was surely sweeping me off of my feet. He was only supposed to be in town for three days.

That first night out, we went out to one of my favorite spots. I took him to PF Chang. That was his first time there, but I helped him order all the right foods. We left there, we went bowling. He said that was his first time bowling in his life and that he truly enjoyed it, even though I beat him. Later on that night, we got back to the Marriott, and the room was filled with red roses, a bottle of champagne, and fresh strawberries. This man was getting more and more impressive by the hour!

That night, we took a bubble bath together. When we got out, he rubbed lotion on every nook and cranny of my body. He laid me on the bed and began to kiss me everywhere – and by everywhere, I do mean *every-where* — which led to us having sex. The sex was immaculate; he was so gentle with me, yet so strong. I felt as if this man was not having sex with me, but that he was making love to me. His skills were a 10+. We fell asleep spooning.

Even though Nasir had money, I didn't want for him to think that was the only reason that I was interested in him, because it wasn't. I played it safe by going to low-key restaurants, not the higher-end places. We would go to the beach, comedy places, and do recreational activities such as bowling, bike riding, paintball, and arcades. I enjoyed every minute that I spent with Nasir. Most of the time, he would only stay for about three days, and then it would be time for him to go. I truly dreaded that.

It had gotten to where every time he was coming into town, he would Western Union me $300 to get a rental. Since I didn't have a credit card at the time, they required me to put that much cash as a deposit. Once I would return the car I would get most of the money back. Instead of going out and spending the money on clothes or shoes, I decided to start saving for a down payment for a car. In addition to me saving that money, Nasir was also giving me money every time he left. It was only like $200. However, within a month and a half's time, I was able to save up $1,200 for a down payment for a car.

When Nasir called to inform me about his next trip, I told him that I would need $1,500 this time. I explained that I saved up some money but that I needed the extra money for a down payment on a car of my own. He said that wouldn't be a problem.

When he got into town, I met him at the Marriott, as usual. When I walked into the room, he was putting money into the hotel room safe. He had to have at least $50,000 sitting in there. He reached in and handed me $2,000.

He said, "That's for the down payment, and *only* spend it on the down payment. You hear me?"

"Yes."

He and I always rented two rental cars, one for him, and one for me. However, when we went out, we would always take his rental. On that night, he decided that we should take two different cars. After we ate dinner at the Stinking Rose, we were driving on La Cienega. When Nasir, pulled over at a gas station, I followed. I pulled up next to his driver's side window and rolled my window down.

"Why did you stop?"

"Go on back to the hotel. I'm meeting someone to drop off something."

"I will just stay with you," I offered. However, he insisted that I leave right that moment.

About 1 ½ hours later, he showed up at the hotel. I asked, "What was that about?"

He said, "I told you I was meeting someone."

"Why did I have to leave?"

He only replied with, "Because."

"Because what?" I pressed.

He said, "Because I am not a producer, I am a drug dealer."

Somehow when he said that, I wasn't astonished. I sat down on the bed and didn't say a word for a good five minutes while he sat there with a look of fear on his face. When I finally broke the silence, the first thing I asked him was, "Why did you lie to me?"

He stated, "I was afraid that you wouldn't want to talk with me anymore if I told you the truth."

I replied, "You could have at least been honest with me and let me decide if this was something that I wanted to get myself into."

He said, "And for that, I am truly sorry. I enjoy spending time with you and doing new and exciting things. You have seen a part of me that few have ever seen. I am enjoying my time with you. Now that you know the truth, what are we going to do?"

I looked at him and said, "Order dessert like we planned."

We ate and fell asleep in each other's arms. I decided to stay with Nasir, not just because of the financial aspects, but because he had also grown on me, and I truly enjoyed everything about our relationship. To a certain extent, though, I was upset with him for not telling me. I thought maybe I needed a break from him to see if I could find something better. I was walking out of the mall one evening when I ran into a guy that stood 5'11" tall, medium build, with a honey-brown complexion.

I heard him say, "What are you doing for dinner tonight?"

I wasn't sure who he was talking to, so I kept walking.

He yelled, "I said, what are you doing for dinner tonight?"

I turned and said, "Are you talking to me?"

"You're the only pretty woman out here I see." A man's flattery will always get him a foot in the door. I smiled so hard that my yellow skin began to blush. He said, "You're blushing."

"Am I?"

He asked, "What's your name?"

"Kennedee. What's yours?"

"Cameron. Would you like to go to dinner with me tonight?"

"Sure!"

We met at the Cheesecake Factory in the Marina. We talked over dinner. He turned out to be a tax accountant that owned a family establishment in Inglewood. He was twenty-eight years old, lived by himself, and had no children. He owned a townhome in the nice part of Inglewood. He sounded like a really good catch. We went out on a few more dates. He seemed a little bit cockier as time went on, but it wasn't to the point that it was annoying to me, so he got a pass.

We had only been seeing one another for a few weeks when he called and asked me a favor. I said, "What do you need?"

"Can you cook?" he asked.

I said, "Yeah, why?"

He explained, "Well, the Superbowl is coming up, and I was thinking that maybe we could host a Superbowl party at my house. You can invite some of your girls, and I will invite some of my boys."

I said, "That sounds like a plan!" I proceeded to get my girls Shelby, Taylor, and Erin together for the party.

The night before the Superbowl party, I met Cameron at his house, and we went to the store to get the items we needed for the party. At the store, we picked up all the fixings to make some tacos.

I ended up spending the night. The next morning, he woke up about eight o'clock. That was early for me, because when I don't attend church on Sundays, I stay in the bed until ten o'clock. He insisted that I get out of bed, and that we go to breakfast before we got the day started. I showered and got dressed. We drove to IHOP for breakfast. We got back from breakfast and we immediately started to clean the house. After we were done, I begin to cut the chicken breasts to sauté, grated the cheese, sliced and diced the tomatoes, onions, cilantro, and lettuce. Once the time came closer for guests to arrive, I started to fry the tortillas. I then began to make batches of pink panties and strawberry margaritas. Everything was ready when the guests began to arrive. We had about ten people in the house, however, only three of them were girls, and seven of them were his boys.

He pulled me to the side and said, "I thought that you were inviting your girls?"

I said, "You told me to invite a few people. I did."

He frowned. "I need you to invite some more girls."

"It's too last minute to invite the rest of the crew, because they already have plans."

He walked away angrily. I asked my girls to come over for a second. They walked into his room, and I closed the door. I explained to them what Cameron had just told me. I said, "He act like he mad or something."

Taylor said, "Don't even trip off of him. What can you do now? He should have told you that from the beginning."

We all walked out of the room and resumed watching the game.

About an hour and a half later, the doorbell started to ring. Within forty-five minutes, about four unidentified women began to walk through the door. My girls were looking at me, wondering what was going on. I had no answer for them. I asked Cameron to come into the room. He walked in and I asked him, "What's up? Who are all these women coming over here?"

"They're just a few friends that I know. They just here to watch the game. Don't trip." He kissed me on the cheek and walked back into the den.

Before I could go back into the den, I was met in the hallway by Shelby. She pulled me into the bathroom and said, "What does he think he is doing?"

I told her, "He said these chicks were just his friends."

She sarcastically said, "Yeah, okay."

I could tell that the women were there because they had an interest in Cameron. As the game proceeded, there were two women in particular that just couldn't seem to keep their hands off of him. I would look over and would see one of them whispering in his ear or looking over at me with the evil eye. This situation was getting out of control very quickly.

My girls could tell I was getting more uncomfortable with every move that was made. Erin and Taylor got up right before the game ended and said they were leaving and to call them later. Shelby had ridden with Erin and Taylor, but she said that she was staying.

As the party began to wind down, Shelby and I begin to clean up the kitchen. When we were done, folks were still there talking and playing cards and dominoes.

Some of the guys began to leave, as well as a few of the females. However, those same two females that I saw talking with Cameron most of the game was still lingering. I sat down at the table where Cameron's best friend Scott was playing.

He looked over and said, "Please don't hurt 'em."

I said, "Why would say that?"

He replied, "It's all over your face. He's not tripping over these girls; he really like you."

I said, "Well, I can't tell!"

The last two of the guys finally left. So now there was just Shelby, Scott, Cameron, the two chicks, and me. I went into the bedroom.

Shelby came in and said, "What is going on? What are they still doing here?"

I sighed. "It's like a standoff - who is going to have him for the night? I am just going to leave." I got my stuff together from the night before, and Shelby and I walked out of the room. When we walked back into the den, Cameron and one of the chicks were missing. Scott and the other chick were still there.

Scott said, "Why you leaving?"

I retorted, "You know why!" I walked out the door.

The remaining chick screamed, "Bye!"

Shelby and I looked at one another and kept walking. We were ready to get it started at that point, but I told her, "Naw, let's just roll, she's not worth it."

We got to the front of the townhouse gates to find Cameron hugging the other chick in a tight in embrace. Shelby yelled, "Hell naw!"

At that moment, Cameron looked and saw us standing there looking at him. The chick quickly got into her car and drove off. Cameron began jogging to my car. I tried to hurry and get in, because I really didn't have anything else to say to him. I had already made up my mind that I was done with him. I thought I was in the clear when I went to shut my door, but there he was grabbing the door to keep it from shutting.

He was out of breath and asked, "Why are you leaving?"

I said, "Seriously? You have to ask?"

He made a face. "What?"

"If for one moment you think that I think these chicks were just some friends, you got me fucked up! How dare you have me throw this party with you, clean your house, and cook food for you to invite some other women over here to entertain? Maybe you should have had them cut up that damn chicken and hand-grate the cheese, and fry the tortilla shells, and play bartender. Where the hell were they when I was doing all this shit? I don't know what you think this is, but you got me fucked up! I don't play that! You have disrespected me to the tenth power, and I'm out."

He said, "Well, be out then, since you want to act like a bitch!" He slammed the door.

I opened my car door back up. "Who you think you calling a bitch? You a bitch for pulling a stunt like this."

"Fuck you then, bitch!"

The word bitch had come out of his mouth one too many times. I was on fire behind how he had treated me. He began to walk back to the gates of the townhouse. His Ford F-150 was parked on the street right behind my car. I started walking to his truck, yelling, "I got your bitch!" I made my way to his driver's side door, turned my back toward the door, and took my right foot and kicked the shit out of his car. All you heard was a loud thump. He just stood there in awe, and then he started to chase me. I had become a track star. I made it in the car and drove off.

Shelby laughed, saying, "That's what that punk gets trying to play someone! He doesn't know who he was messing with."

"He does now! Good riddance to him!"

I was never the forgiving type once you pissed me off. Cameron called me days later to apologize, but I wasn't having it. He blatantly disrespected me, and for that, he could not be forgiven. He wasn't worth all that.

Man, my luck with men. I thought I should just stick with Nasir. At least I knew what to expect from him, knew his situation, and there were perks that came with it.

By spring, Nasir's trips to California were not as often as they were in the beginning. It was okay though, because every month, he still sent me an allowance via

Western Union. With that money, I was still able to go out and have a good time with my girls to kill the time until he returned. I missed him very much, yet we still talked every day.

I had a big birthday party that summer at Keyshawn Johnson's restaurant Reign in Beverly Hills. Though Nasir didn't make it, he sent enough money to make sure that my friends and I had a marvelous time. I had a fabulous party, but I would rather have had him there. By this time, I was growing tired of waiting for him to come back to California. Though he offered me many trips to fly to come see him, I was afraid of flying.

A week after my birthday, Nasir told me that he was flying in to Las Vegas, and that he wanted me to meet him there. He explained that this was an extension of my birthday gift from him. I told him, "You know I don't fly!"

He said, "Well, drive down."

I had been to Las Vegas before, but never by myself. I sat on the phone for a second contemplating whether or not I should go. I finally decided. "What the hell, I will meet you there." I called in sick the next day and I hit the 15 freeway, driving all the way to Las Vegas by myself. It took me approximately 4 ½ hours to get there, and during my ride, I spoke with various people via phone. Many people were concerned about me driving so far alone. To be honest, I wasn't scared. The sense of scariness was replaced by the excitement of seeing Nasir.

When I arrived in Las Vegas, he was already at the hotel waiting for me in a penthouse suite. He bought me a whole new wardrobe for the weekend that included beautiful dresses, swimwear, shoes, lingerie, jewelry, and designer handbags. All I could say was wow! I never thought in a million years that he would have this waiting for me. It was more than I could have ever expected. That weekend, we went to the nicest restaurants. We went to the hottest clubs. We shopped at the finest stores. I had the time of my life with this man.

Our final day, he sat me down and told me that he had something to tell me. I thought he was going to ask me to marry him. But the keyword was "tell" not "ask". He explained, "The reason my visits to California stopped becoming so frequent is because the feds busted me. I only have a few months until it's time for me to turn myself in. I got myself a lawyer to fight the case, and they ended up taking a plea bargain. Instead of ten years, I got sentenced to eight years."

I can't even explain the hurt that I began to feel. It was such a sad situation. Although Nasir was committing illegal activities that got him into trouble, I still was very saddened that this man that had done so much for me within a short period of time was going to jail. I was going to keep it real. Even though he had done a lot for me, there was no way in hell that I was putting my life on hold for him for eight years.

Once he returned back home, I didn't hear from him. However, I still wanted to be a good friend and keep in touch with him, because I truly appreciated everything that he had ever done for me. I had an old address for him where I had sent pictures to him. I sent a letter stating that I needed for someone to get in touch with me and let me know his whereabouts. In the letter, I included my number for someone to call.

A few weeks later, the phone rang, and the caller ID showed a number from New York state. When I answered and said hello, there was a female voice on the other line. She said that her name was Arlene and that she was Nasir's baby mama. She went on to let me know that she had been with him since they were sixteen years old, and that they lived together and had a daughter together. She said that she wasn't surprised that he had someone else in another state. She told me that she was done with Nasir and that she was taking her daughter and moving to Maryland, purchasing a brick home (I think I was supposed to be impressed when she said a *brick* home) and that she was done with him. She said, "I'll let Nasir know that you're looking for him."

When I got off the phone with her, somehow I wasn't shocked that this was happening. I never thought that he was cheating on me, but I never thought that this was going on either. At that time in my life, I had come to expect the unexpected. That way, when it happened, I wouldn't be so hurt. I will say it did sting me, but I wasn't hurt.

A few weeks went by. I never received a phone call from Nasir, but then, I knew his baby mama was going to be a hater and not forward my letter or message to him. Over the years, the Internet had become my best friend, and I ended up finding him on the inmate locator website. All I had to do was put in his name, race, and date of birth. All his information popped up: name, inmate number, and location of the correctional facility. I know you're probably thinking, "Why in the hell is she looking for this jailbird?"

Have you ever had the feeling to reciprocate when someone does something for you? I could have easily walked away from this situation, yet I felt compelled to be there for a man that had been there for me. I don't agree with Nasir's tactics of how he generated his income, yet he had a good heart. This man took care of me in more ways than one. He didn't have to, but he did, and that's the part of me that loves him to this day. In the first letter that I sent him, I shared the same thoughts that I just shared with you. In addition to the letter, I sent a separate envelope to another address with a $100 money order to put money on his books.

Throughout the years, he and I have kept in touch via mail and phone while he is serving out the rest of his sentence in Ohio. Every two months, I would send him $100 for his books. He and I now know that what we once had will never be, yet we have a mutual level of respect and love for one another. In our phone conversations, I speak with him about my newfound relationships. In turn, he offers tips on how to keep the men that I date and gives advice about what to do with the wrong ones.

He has moved on with his life as I have. I guess Arlene truly washed her hands of him, because Nasir now has a girlfriend named Sara that has been down with him since his second year of serving his sentence. He says he plans to marry her when he gets out in August of 2010. If he does marry Sara, I hope that he invites me so that I can be there to wish them all the love, happiness and joy in the world. He has been so good to me, even behind prison walls, and I am so glad to have met him and for him to be a part of my life. I am glad that I can call him a friend. Even if he didn't turn out to be my Prince Charming, he would be the closest thing to it for many years.

Jackson – He's Back

Sometimes, all it takes is one time to see someone that you truly cared, loved, or lusted for to set it all off again. This was the case when I saw Jackson one night while I was out. He and I ran into each other while out at the club. He was still fine as hell, and with one look at me, he still could get my panties wet. When he spotted me, he tried to play like he wasn't fazed that he had seen me. I went ahead with his game, but by the end of the night, I ignored him so well he couldn't help but try to get my attention. We ended up hooking up later on that night at a hotel, where we had the head-board knocking for hours. It was just like old times. Jackson always knew how to please me in every way.

Three months into renewing our relationship, he confessed that he had a girlfriend. I was shocked, because the previous week, we had just spent Valentine's Day together. I was totally hurt that once again, someone else had his heart. I asked, "What made you finally come clean?"

He said, "The two of us are going to be moving in together."

I was crushed, yet there was a part of me that still wanted to be with him. I told him, "I can't see you anymore, since you have a girlfriend."

"I understand," he replied, "but I still want to be with you."

"As much as I care about you, I can't fathom the idea of having to share you with someone else," I told him.

Loneliness will drive you to do some strange things, things that you would never think of doing. Well, that's exactly how this situation got restarted. I ended up calling him nine months later, only because I didn't have anyone else to be with at the time. When I paged him with my cell phone number and my pager code, he called me right back.

"I thought you weren't going to call me anymore since I have a girlfriend," Jackson said as soon as I answered the phone.

I could only sit there and say, "Well, can't a girl change her mind?"

He asked, "Can we meet up later on this weekend?"

And that's exactly what we did. We met up and we talked, and that ended up leading to passionate sex.

He and I were like addicts to one another. We just couldn't get enough of each other no matter how hard we tried. There was just some type of chemistry between us that couldn't be denied. We began to spend quality time with one another, more than we had ever done before. Many times I felt guilty, knowing that Jackson had a girlfriend, but I had been with him for so long that I couldn't let go. While we were together, he would talk about many things, one of them being his girlfriend. He shared her likes, dislikes, lifestyle, and background. Also, anything else that was bothering him about her, he would discuss with me. He told me that she and I shared many physical attributes and characteristics. I can see why he liked the girl then - ha-ha! She reminded him of me.

The more time that he and I began to spend with one another, I could tell that his feelings had grown for me over the years. One day, I decided to text him and ask him how he felt about me. His reply was "I love you."

I was astonished when I saw the text, but somehow, I knew deep down inside that despite everything that he and I had been through, he loved me in some kind of way. I was so excited that he had finally opened up his feelings to me that I had to call everybody and tell them what he said. Many people were not shocked that he had finally confessed his love for me, because we had been through so much. It had to be love, or just pure craziness. Looking back, it was a bit of both.

After he told me that, I couldn't wait to see him again. I wanted to finally hear those words come out of his mouth in person and be able to tell him the same thing, because I truly did love him. Days later, we met at Dockweiler Beach. I loved to go to the beach, even though it was a cold day in February. He brought a blanket and we sat there on the shore and watched the waves flow by. It was so cold that we stayed warm by hugging in each other's arms, enjoying the scenery.

He started to kiss me gently on my cheek. His lips inched toward my mouth while he suddenly grabbed my hair, then kissed me long and hard. His tongue felt like fire. He stopped kissing me, gazed into my eyes, and whispered, "Kennedee, I love you."

I whispered softly, "Jackson, I love you too."

He opened up himself to me, and I opened up myself to him. Deep down, I knew this love triangle wasn't going to last long. He would have to eventually choose if he wanted his girlfriend Shay or me. I made the mistake of allowing him to have his cake and eat it too, and it was now going to be a mess to clear up.

I was at home one Sunday evening when the phone rang. When I answered, the person on the other line hung up. Call it ESP, but in the back of my mind, I knew it was Shay. About fifteen minutes later, the phone rang again. I said, "Hello?"

This time there was a male voice on the other end of the line. "What's your name?"

"You called here. Why don't you tell me who you are looking for, and I will see if I can help you," I huffed.

He said, "Well, I met this girl about two months ago, and I was trying to see if it was her. Where do you live at?"

I thought to myself, *This fool is an amateur!* He definitely wasn't very clever in his approach. I said, "Well, you still haven't told me who you are looking for. Where exactly did the girl say she lived?"

He stated, "She said in Glendora."

"No, you have the wrong person." I hung up. I already knew what it was about. Shay had finally found my number somewhere and she wanted to know who I was. I knew she had put some guy she knew up to calling me to pump me for information, but I was already a pro at that game, so she couldn't get that one past me.

I guess the information that I did or didn't give wasn't good enough, because about ten minutes later, the phone clicked while I was on the other line with my girl

Neena. I was explaining to her what was going on, because I knew the ish was about to hit the fan. When I heard the phone click I told Neena I would call her back. When I clicked over, I said, "Hello?"

The female voice on the other line said, "Um, yes, this is Jackson's girlfriend."

I interrupted her before she could go any further. "Shay, how can I help you?"

She was astounded that I knew her name. She quickly asked, "How did you know my name?"

I said, "I know everything about you. I know that you go to Cal State Dominguez Hills majoring in Sociology. I know that you are twenty-three years old. I know that you work at Sears. Now what else would you like to know about me?"

There was a slight pause. She hesitantly asked, "How long have you and Jackson been seeing each other?"

I answered honestly. "Off and on for the last six years. He and I have a bond that can't be broken. He even told me that he loved me."

After that, she wanted to know small details like my name, how old I was, where I lived. She was on a need-to-know basis, so I told her what she needed to know and made up the rest. She must have seen that I was reluctant, so she made her way off the phone. As soon as we hung up, I called Jackson. When he picked up the phone, I said, "Your girl just got done calling here questioning me. I'm sure she will be calling you soon."

He said, "What did you tell her?"

"Everything."

He sounded frustrated. "Why didn't you call me so I could tell you what to say?"

"I didn't know there was a script I had to go by."

He paused. "My line is buzzing; let me call you back.
Later on that night, I got a phone call from him. He
was upset with me. He asked me how I could lie to her. I
replied, "About what?"

"Everything that you told her was a lie!"

At that point, I knew she had to be on the phone. So I
began to point out the obvious, like if I was lying, how
did I know her name, where she went to school, where
she works, and how old she is? I told him, "Don't even
try to play me like that! Don't be mad at me because you
got caught. You never gave me a script of what to say or
not say, therefore, I told the truth. The rest falls on you. I
know what you are trying to do, and I know she is on the
phone."

Shay spoke up, "I am on the phone, you lying bitch!"

I said, "I can be all the bitches you want, but what it
boils down to is that you are going to stay with him no
matter what you believe. If you choose to stay, that's on
you, but know that any time I want your man, I can have
him. Right now, he is just mad at me because he is
caught. Trust me when I say I could call him next week,
next month, or next year, and whenever I call, he will
come running."

She yelled, "Fuck you, bitch!" The line went dead.

I guess the truth hurt. But it was the truth. No matter
where we were in life, I knew that I could always call
Jackson and he would be there in a blink of an eye.

A few weeks went by. I hadn't heard anything from
him. I was feeling tired and nauseated so I went to the
doctor, only to find out I was two months pregnant. I
was so displeased with myself to be in this situation. I got
in the car and bawled my eyes out. This pregnancy
couldn't have come at a worse time. After I gathered my

composure, I reached for my cell phone and called Jackson. He didn't answer, so I just left him a message stating that I was pregnant and that I needed to speak with him. I'm sure the first thing that went through his mind that it was just a ploy to get him to call back, but unfortunately, this was a real situation that wasn't going to go away.

He didn't return my call. I attempted to call him several days in a row, and there was still no answer. I knew that it was time to go to drastic measures. I turned to a people search website on the Internet, where I was able to obtain his current address and home phone number. I called the number, and Shay answered. I said, "Hi, may I speak with Jackson?"

She asked, "Who's calling?"

I said, "Kennedee."

She shouted, "You won't be speaking to him on this line, bitch!" Then she hung up.

At this point, I knew things were about to get ugly. All I wanted to do was sit down with him and discuss our options, but since he wanted to act like a dumb ass, he left me no other choice. I called my girl Kali. She and Jackson never did get along. She didn't like him because she didn't appreciate the way things went down, and he didn't like her because he knew she always had my back no matter what. I picked her up and we headed to Long Beach. We arrived at the address that the website had provided me. I wasn't awed by the neighborhood. Let's just say it's somewhere you shouldn't have been after the streetlights came on. Kali and I got out of the car and made our way up the stairs to their apartment door.

I stood off to the side while Kali knocked on the door. She knocked once, and no one answered. She knocked again, and this time the door opened. I could see the surprised look on Jackson's face as he saw Kali standing there. He immediately came out of the doorway and looked to the left, where he spotted me.

Jackson said, "Damn!"

I said, "Damn is right! Now bring your ass outside!"

"Let me grab my jacket."

Kali said, "I hope you do come back out here!"

He looked at her and rolled his eyes. He did come back outside, however…with Shay. Shay was not at all what I had pictured in my head. She was light-skinned with medium-length hair, an average build, and she was short. Hell, she didn't even look twenty-three - more like thirty-three and she didn't look a damn thing like me.

Shay screamed, "I'm going to call the police and my people if you don't leave!"

I shot back, "Call the police, I don't care! I've been to jail before, bitch!"

She went back to the house screaming, "I got my family on their way!"

I screamed back, "I hope they get here before the police do so we can all go to jail together!" (Y'all know I didn't want to go back to jail, I was just selling woof tickets).

Jackson asked, "Can I talk to you over here?"

Kali said, "No, you can't pull her nowhere! She stays right here! Say what you have to say."

Jackson said, "Really, did you have to come over here?"

I rolled my eyes. "You left me no choice with you avoiding me. You left me to figure it out for myself."

He said, "I would have eventually called you."

"Eventually!" I yelled. "I don't have time to waste with you!"

"How did find out where I lived?"

"Don't worry about all that, just know that I'm here."

Jackson glared at me. "You know I will never forgive you for this."

Kali interjected, "Who gives a fuck! If you would have manned up, no one would have to come over here in the first place!"

He said under his breath, "I never did like your ass!"

She said, "What did you just say? You wanna repeat that again?" Thank God the police had pulled up! See, Kali is about six feet tall and she wasn't afraid to smack the ish out of Jackson. The police got out of their car. As they approached us, one officer asked, "What seems to be the problem?"

Shay came out of the house yelling, "She is trespassing and harassing us, and she needs to go!"

I told the police, "I was just in the neighborhood, and I stopped to chat with him."

They looked at Jackson and asked, "Is this true?" He just looked like he was scared to talk. The officer turned to me and said, "Well, Miss, if you could just say your goodbyes, we can all be on our way."

"Fine. See ya soon, Jackson." He knew what I meant. That night I vowed to Kali that I was going to do something to get him back. Wasn't quite sure what, but I knew I couldn't let him slide. That vindictive spirit was hard to tame.

Before I could even conjure up a plan, about a week later, I was at work when I had to go to the bathroom. I was bleeding. Not a little, but a whole lot. I quickly left work to go the nearest emergency room. On the way there, I already knew that I was losing the baby, but I was hoping that the doctor would tell me something different. When I arrived at the emergency room, they took me in right away. The doctor did an examination and told me that I indeed was having a miscarriage. The only thing that I could do was wait for the baby to pass at this point, and once the baby passed, I would have to come back to the hospital to get rechecked. I was mortified that this was all they were going to do for me. I just cried on my way home. When I got there, I just got in the bed.

Later that evening, I began to have cramping. When I went to use the bathroom, I heard a thump in the toilet, and I knew what it was. It took me a few hours to come to the realization that I had just lost a child. As I sat there, I begin to have severe cramping, worse than any menstrual cramps that I had ever had before. I started sweating, feeling nauseated and dizzy. I called Neena to come get me, and she drove me to the hospital.

I explained to the ER doctor what had happened. He began to run tests. The pain was so bad that I was administered morphine, and still the pain just didn't seem to go away. I was half out of it when the doctor came back hours later to let me know that I was going to be staying overnight for observation. Neena started making phone calls to my family and friends to let them know that I was in the hospital.

My cousin Derwin must have called Jackson, because out of the blue, he called the hospital. You could hear the concern in his voice. He wanted to know how I was holding up. He asked if I wanted him to come. As much as I wanted for him to come, I needed for him to stay away. He continued to call during my three-day stay in hospital. Turns out I had fibroids, and the doctors thought they were going to have to do an emergency surgery. I ended up being fine, but I was taken off of work for two weeks to recuperate. After Jackson found out I wasn't going to die, his shoulder turned cold, and the phone calls stopped. I guess he was still trying to be mad. Who cared? He was mad, but he was guilty as much as I was for all this chaos.

Reese – You Say She's Just A Friend

C lubbing was never my cup of tea, and going on Crenshaw was no longer an alternative as far as meeting men on the scene. Steve Harvey had a segment on his radio show called the dating game. One day I overheard him announce for people to send in their name and bio's. I thought to myself, *What the heck, why not?* I have nothing to lose. I sent the bio over in November of 2004. They didn't call me until January 2005. I went on the show, and I had never heard Steve Harvey give the participant's full name. When he announced me, he gave my full name, Kennedee Devoe. I thought to myself, *Oh Lord, now everybody and they mama going to know I am up here trying to get a date.* It didn't matter anyway, because the moment I opened my mouth, anyone that knew me from elementary up would know it was me. I have a very, very distinctive voice. I discussed what I was looking for and what I wasn't looking for in a man. There were three callers that called in to get a date with me. The first prospect sounded promising, but after listening to the other two, I decided to get with that one. We were set to go out that night to Color Me Mine and the Water Grill in downtown LA.

I ended up getting a call from one of the radio station's representatives. He said that my date cancelled, so they were setting me up with one of the other respondents, number three, who wasn't even in the running. I knew right there I should have cancelled, but I went with the flow. I arrived back at the radio station at 6:00 p.m. to get chauffeured in a limo for our date.

There my date stood, frumpy and unattractive, with one rose in his hand. He asked, "Are you Kennedee?"

I felt like saying, "Hell no!" and running like Flo Jo. Instead, I said, "And you are?" This is how uninterested I was, because I can't even remember his name. When the limo driver opened the door, I told him to skip Color Me Mine and take us straight to dinner. The driver obliged.

When we arrived, all I wanted to do was eat and get out of there. He could tell I wasn't interested, yet he tried to make conversation. As he talked about himself, I realized we had absolutely NOTHING in common. So I asked, "What made you call in for the date?"

He said, "I heard the end of the interview, and you said you like scrapbooking, and it made me think of my mom. So I called."

I thought to myself, *Are you freaking serious?* I rolled my eyes in the back of my head.

He said, "What's wrong?"

I stated, "So let me get this straight: you didn't even hear the entire interview, and that one thing prompted you to call?"

With a stupid look on his face, he said "Yes."

That was the end of the date. I told the driver, "Look, don't take the scenic route. Hurry up and get me back to my car."

When we got back to the radio station, my date tried to hug me. Ugh! I said, "I don't know you like that, so let's just shake hands."

He did as I requested and said, "Good night."

The next morning, I was supposed to go back for the follow-up interview. I decided that since the date was a bust, I didn't feel like driving all the way down there for that. The radio station called me that morning, asking where I was, and I told them I wasn't coming in. They decided to do the follow-up over the phone. It was a three-way call with me, Steve Harvey, and the date.

Steve asked, "How did your date go?"

I said, "It was nice."

Steve asked the guy, "What did you think of Kennedee when you saw her?"

"She was very pretty," he answered.

Steve asked, "What did you think of him?"

"He was nice," I replied. Hell, I really didn't have anything nice to say about this date, but I was trying to be nice.

Steve asked, "So did you all enjoy the outing?"

I said, "The food was good."

"What did you eat?"

I can't remember what the guy stated, but I said, "The salmon, and it was good."

Sheryl Underwood was on the show that morning. She said, "Kennedee, let me ask you a question. Did you enjoy the man or the salmon more?"

I said, "The salmon!" She started busting up laughing. However, my answer turned into Steve giving me a lecture on the radio about how women are always saying they want a good man, but yet want to be picky. I didn't agree with his statement, because I have a right to be picky. I know what I like and what I don't like, and this man definitely wasn't it.

So I turned to the new age of dating: I went looking for love on the internet, new-millennium style. I went on a website specifically designed for African-Americans only. I'm not into the jungle fever thing. I've always preferred African-American men, and I found a whole bunch on this website. They had it all, and when I say all, I mean *all*: from tall ones to short ones, from ugly ones to attractive ones, from athletic to more-to-love. You name it, they had your variety, and they were all on there looking for love—supposedly.

I went on a few dates. Many of them made very nice gestures trying to lure me in, but unfortunately, none of them that I met off of this website were truly looking to settle down or looking for love. They were looking for sexual encounters or non-relationships with perks in- volved. Now don't get me wrong, there is nothing wrong with a sexual relationship with perks involved. But I wanted something more, with a commitment involved.

I might be downplaying the situation, as I actually went out on twenty dates within a four month time span. I figured I would get my money's worth. I mean, I had to pay to be on the website anyways. I met so many differ- ent guys and can't even go into detail about all those dates. That would take a whole 'nother book to write. So instead, I'll just move on to the last person that I dated off of the website. His name was Reese. He was chocolate with the nicely-toned athletic body of a runner. He was kind of on the skinny side though, and somewhat of a nerd, but he seemed pretty cool over the phone, so I thought I would finally meet him in person.

When I finally met him, it was at the house of a friend of his in Anaheim. It was game night and they had appetizers, drinks, and lots of games. His friends seemed somewhat cool, and I enjoyed the night, but I would rather have had a one-on-one date so I could get him out of his element. A few weeks later, we did end up going on a date with just the two of us. We walked through the park, he bought me some ice cream, and we talked. Turned out he was a computer geek. He actually worked for some website company as their Information Technology guy. He had a bachelor's degree, his own place, and he didn't have any children—all of the three qualities that I was looking for at that moment. The only thing was, he was broke because he was living outside of his means. He had debt from student loans, and on top of that, he liked to gamble (though I didn't know about the gambling addiction until later). I don't like broke guys because they can't do too much for you. I took a chance on him anyways, despite the fact that I knew how I like to be treated.

Reese seemed to compensate for not having money by doing nice things for me, like cooking. One night, he cooked steak and potatoes, made a salad, and added his specialty dessert, banana pudding. I'm no fan of banana pudding, but I went ahead and ate it, and I must say I was very delighted by the taste of it. Later on that evening, we watched movies, because he had an extensive movie collection - over 300 videos to choose from. I guess when you don't have that much money, you have to indulge in the things that can entertain you best, and movies were his thing. After about two movies, I ended up falling asleep on the couch. We definitely enjoyed each other's company.

I was there five days out of the week. I would leave from work and go straight to his house and go from his house to work. I was there so much that I barely went home. I would just keep a bag full of clothes and spend the whole week with him. He was a cool guy. I really liked him, and the greatest part about him was that he wasn't pressuring me for sex. Every Wednesday, he would have a card game at his house.

He would invite his friends and coworkers and they'd play poker for money. He might lose a lot of times, and a lot of times he would win, but he also would spend some of his weekends at the local casino, which bothered me a little. See, it's one thing to have poker night at your house, but then when you start going to the casino and gambling on a regular basis…to me, that is a sign of a problem…a gambling problem.

His addiction to gambling had gotten so bad he had to get a roommate. When I brought this to his attention, he said that he didn't have a problem. As always, people that have a problem never admit that they do. It's only in the end when they're ready to give up the problem that they admit that they have one, especially when they are in denial. Or they have to lose everything to realize they had a problem. Either way, his denial let me know that he was not ready to give up his gambling addiction. I was good with that. I mean, he wasn't a bad person and he was cool to kick it with, and it wasn't like I was trying to marry him or something. He was considered good for passing time until something better came along.

He told me before that his best friend was a girl by the name of Charlene, and I never really thought too much of it because I have a male best friend as well as a female best friend. But I also know that with my male best friend, I have never ever given him a kiss, had sex with him, or never thought about crossing the line with him. That's why we're still friends to this day.

One night, on Reese's weekly poker night, I dropped by, and Charlene happened to be there. I wasn't at all intimidated by her. She was a little chunky. She was probably about 5'7", and she had buck teeth and bad skin. Not to say that if she was a cute girl that I would've been intimidated, because a lot of times guys will mess with an ugly girl as fast as they'll mess with the cute girl, but the point was that I was not intimidated by her. There was nothing about her that made me feel like I needed to be concerned.

When I walked into the room, I said, "Hello, every-one!" When I looked at her to see if she was going to say hello, she looked up and didn't say a word, then put her head back down.

I went into Reese's room and closed the door, as I always did when he had poker night at his house. I never wanted to bother him or ask questions about how to play the game because I actually could care less about the game. I was so peeved at this chick, because her body language said it all when I walked into the room. After entering his room, I found a little girl that looked like the mini version of Charlene sitting at Reese's computer desk. I asked her, "What's your name?"

She said, "I'm Caprice!"

"Nice to meet you, Caprice, I'm Kennedee, Reese's friend."

"My mom already told me about you."

"Is that right?" I was thinking, *What does that mean?* "I'm going to turn on the TV and lay down, but you can continue to be on the computer."

About thirty minutes later, Charlene walked into the room. She said, "Caprice, it's time to go." Never once did Charlene say, "Hi, it was a pleasure to meet you" or "Have a good night." She said absolutely nothing to me. She just grabbed her daughter, jacket, and purse and walked out the door. From that moment on, I knew she and I weren't going to get along. I don't know why, and I could only speculate at that moment, but I knew that it was definitely going to be a problem. That whole scenario made me think that something more happened between her and Reese before I stepped into the picture, and now with me around, her chances of getting back with him had lessened.

About two weeks later, Reese and I ended up picking up Caprice and taking her to go shopping for a Mother's Day present for Charlene. We went to the mall, and Caprice picked up a sweat suit for her mother. However, she didn't know what size her mother wore. She asked me what size she thought I should get her mom. I recalled in my mind the night that I met her, and I could imagine her wearing a size large.

We all went to dinner that evening, and after dinner, we dropped off Caprice. About two days later I received a call from Reese asking me if I had purposely picked out the wrong size for Charlene's sweat suit, because Charlene said that she couldn't fit it. She didn't know why I would think she wore a large.

I said, "I don't even know her like that! Why would I want to purposely pick out the wrong size for her?"

Reese sighed. "I don't know, but that's what she called and said."

"You believe everything that she says?"

"No, but I'm just saying what she told me."

"What difference does it make that it was the wrong size? She can take it back. Let's not make a big deal out of it." I hung up the phone. I was so pissed off at the fact that she thought I was trying to intentionally get her the wrong size. Who does that? I could see that she was definitely being more than just a little catty.

A couple of days after that conversation had taken place, I asked him if he and Charlene had ever slept together, and he swore up and down that nothing ever happened between the two, that they were just friends and had only been friends, that he had actually met her while she was pregnant with Caprice. A friend had introduced them, and they just decided to just be friends. That got me to thinking. Charlene probably wanted to hook up with Reese, but the timing was off. She was pregnant, she knew it wasn't going down, so she settled for just being a friend. I could relate to that scenario. After all, I met Garin while I was pregnant, and I put him in the friend category even though I knew I liked him. So I was thinking that maybe over the years, she started to like him more, but it was too late because they only turned out to be friends.

Reese had told me that Charlene asked if it was okay for her to have Caprice's 10th birthday party at his house. He was the only person she knew that had a pool, and she wanted it to be a pool party. How convenient! She wanted it to be held on Memorial Day, and she would be supplying all the food, drinks, and entertainment. Caprice's friends from school would be attending, and a few of Charlene's family members would also be there.

I told him, "I already have plans for that day."

He shrugged. "No worries. I'm not sure you were invited anyway."

My mouth dropped open in shock. "What?"

"Well, being that it's a kid's party…"

"Uh huh… Well, can I come by after the party is over on Monday to spend the night?"

He smiled. "Okay."

So as I had planned, I went to the Reggae Festival at UCLA, like I do every year. I went with my girls Shelby and Arianna. We would normally stay until the end of the festival, however, I ran into Jackson while we were there. He still looked pissed and didn't speak to me, so I decided that maybe we should leave a little earlier than usual. We went over to Magic Johnson's Friday's to grab something to eat, and afterward, Shelby and I drove over to Reese's house. He had asked me to bring a friend with me because a few of his single friends were there.

I rang the doorbell, and Reese answered the door. He greeted me with a hug and I introduced him to Shelby. Shelby and Reese started to make small talk, so I began to make my way to his bedroom. After passing the dining room area, I heard Reese yell, "Kennedee, let me talk with you real quick!"

I stopped and turned. "What's up?"

He whispered quietly in my ear, "Charlene and Caprice are in my bed laying down. They are going to spend the night because Charlene was too tired to drive home."

"Too tired! She only lives twenty minutes away from here!"

Reese shrugged. "Well, they are in there asleep."

"Asleep? It's only nine o'clock! Are you serious?"

"Yes."

"Well, have a good night," I huffed. I told Shelby, "Come on, let's go."

As Shelby and I walked back to her car, I discussed with her how this was some bull-ish about this chick. "She is just spending the night because she knew I was coming over! I really think that these two have done the do before, or she wants to do the do with him."

Shelby said, "I have no doubt that you will get down to the bottom of this situation."

I sighed. "To be honest, I wasn't really concerned until she just pulled this stunt, but if he is doing something or has done something with her, the truth will come to light." Shelby and I hugged each other, got into our separate cars, and drove home.

The next day, Reese called my phone several times, but I didn't answer. I was totally pissed with him for allowing this girl to pull a move like that. He finally left a voicemail and he apologized, but the part that got me was when he said, "You could have stayed and slept on the couch with me."

What did he just say? I could have slept on the couch? What I look like sleeping on the couch while some other woman who is not his mother, sister, or anything blood-related lies in his bed? I don't think so!

He called for a few days, and I still didn't answer. A week had gone by when I received a blocked call. It was Reese. He offered to take me to dinner, but I declined. I seized the moment to ask what I had been dying to know, hoping that he would finally tell the truth. "Is there anything going on between you and Charlene?"

"I thought we had this conversation."

I said, "We somewhat did, but I just find it suspect that she just had to spend the night. Do you think that she's jealous of our relationship?"

He said, "No, Charlene has a man."

"I can't tell!" I retorted.

He promised he wouldn't let Charlene come in between us again.

A few weeks had passed, and we didn't have any more issues with buck-tooth Charlene. Things were back to normal with us and we were enjoying each other's company. His birthday was coming up, and I asked him what he would like to do.

"I'm not sure, but I'll let you know."

I found that to be an odd answer, but everyone celebrates their birthday differently. A few days before his birthday, I approached him again with the question of what he would like to do.

"Actually, I am having a party," Reese admitted.

"When were you going to tell me? Where's the party going to be?"

"Right there at the house."

"What time?"

Reese said, "Well, I don't know if you can come."

"What do you mean you don't know if I can come!" I shouted.

"Well, Charlene is the one throwing the party, and she sent out the invites."

"So?"

"Well, I don't know," he said, avoiding the issue.

"What kind of answer is 'I don't know'? Let me get this straight: Charlene is throwing a party for you at YOUR house, and you don't know if I can come? You sound real stupid right now! What is Charlene's problem?" Reese just sat there like a bump on a log. "Well, if you don't tell me, maybe she will!" I grabbed the house phone, and then I went searching in the bedroom for his cell phone. I found the cell, looked up Charlene's number, and called from the house phone. He sat there with a dumb look on his face as I stood over him making the call. The phone rang a few times before she finally answered.

"What's up?"

"Hey, Charlene, this is Kennedee, how are you?"

"How can I help you?" she asked warily.

See, I was trying to be nice, yet she still had an attitude. I said, "I was calling because Reese told me that you plan on giving him a birthday party."

"Yeah, and...?" she shot back.

"Well, I was just wondering why I hadn't received a birthday invite."

Charlene laughed. "Because you aren't invited!"

"Excuse me?"

"You heard me!"

I calmly said, "How the hell you think that you are going to have a party over here and think that I am not going to be here?"

She said, "Watch!" and then hung up the phone on me.

I put down the phone and said, "Reese, this bitch has got me fucked up to think that it's about to go down like that!"

He asked, "Why did you even call her?"

I yelled, "Because you need to grow some fucking balls and stop letting this buck-tooth chick try and run what we are doing over here!" The house phone began to ring. I looked at the caller ID, and it was Charlene calling back. I said, "It's your *friend*. You want me to answer, or do you want to get it?"

He snatched the phone out of my hand and answered. I could hear Charlene yelling and screaming at the top of her lungs. I went and picked up the other phone. Just as I picked up, I heard her say, "I am coming over there, and I am going to fuck that bitch up!"

I interrupted, "Well, I will be right here waiting for you!"

She screamed, "Reese, you are letting her listen to the conversation too? Me and you are going to have problems when I get there!" She hung up.

I didn't think too much about her coming over there because it was a Sunday night at almost ten o'clock at night. She was a single mother, and I sure didn't think that she would drag her ten-year-old daughter out for some bull-ish like that.

Reese just sat on the couch in disbelief that all this was happening. I said, "Well don't just sit there; say something!"

He said, "Why did you have to call her? You know she's going to come over here now."

"Do you think I care? You act as if she is your girlfriend instead of me!"

"I told you before that nothing happened between us!" he exclaimed.

"Oh, so she's acting like a psycho chick for nothing? I find that hard to believe."

Reese's eyes darted around. "We need to leave."

"For what."

"Because she's coming over here."

"So what!" I yelled. "Am I supposed to be scared or something? She can bring her ass over here if she wants to."

Around twenty minutes later, he said go with me down to the carport. I said, "Why do I need to go with you?"

"Because I need to get something out of the car and I don't want you here by yourself if she comes."

"I'm not scared!" I scoffed.

"I know you not, but I would feel better if you went with me."

"Fine!" I huffed.

We walked down to the carport and he started looking in his car for whatever he came down for. I turned my back to the car for a second to look at something. When I turned back around, he was gone.

I slowly made my way back to his townhouse, but I was pissed off that he left me out there by myself. As I approached the east side of the townhouse, I could hear Charlene yelling at Reese. I thought to myself, *This punk timed it just right where I would be out of the house at the time she arrived!*

Charlene was yelling, "How dare you have her call me? What the fuck is wrong with you? Why would you do something like this to me? Don't you have any regards for my feelings?" She was asking him lots of questions, yet she wasn't giving him time to answer. She finally stated, "You better have gotten her ass out of here before I came!"

Whoops!!! That was my cue. I yelled through the front door, "I didn't go anywhere, bitch, I am standing right here on the porch!"

I could hear her yelling, saying, "She still here? She is still here?"

I began banging on the door, telling Reese he better let me in. He opened the door halfway. I could see her standing in the dining room. I started yelling, "I thought you were going to fuck me up, Charlene! I ain't no punk! Don't let the pretty face fool you. I will get in that ass, bitch! You better just stand there and act like you don't hear me. Talking all that shit over the phone, and you ain't got nothing to say now!"

She all of a sudden turned and started making her way to the door. Reese stood in between us as we attempted to deliver fist blows to one another. Reese yelled to his roommate Dre to come help. Caprice began yelling, "Mommy, no, please don't get hurt!"

For a moment I thought, *Ooh my, she brought her daughter along with her?* That's not a good look. I mean, if you are going to go cause some drama, please leave the child at home or drop her off over your mama's house. She definitely wasn't setting a good example for her daughter.

Dre grabbed Charlene and Reese grabbed me. Reese took me outside while Charlene remained inside. He said, "You gotta go."

"Trust me, I would have been gone right after you left me outside, but your dumb ass forgot to tell me to get my keys and purse, you dumb fuck!"

"Why would you do all that, knowing that Caprice was there?" Reese asked.

"How the hell was I supposed to know that her ghetto ass would bring along her daughter in the middle of the night?"

He and I sat by the pool for about twenty minutes. The whole time, I insisted that we return to the house so that I could get my belongings. He kept saying, "I am trying to make sure she is gone."

"For her sake or mine?" I asked. He had no reply. Finally, I had enough. I said, "I am going to go get my stuff, and you better hope she isn't there!"

We walked in the house, and the only person that was there was Dre. He said she had left right after the fight was broken up. I went into the bedroom. Reese said, "You can stay the night if you want."

I said, "Please! I can't stand the sight of you right now! I am out, and you don't have to worry about me coming back!"

He tried to apologize as I walked to my car, but I wasn't having it. This was straight bull-ish. A few days later, my phone rang about 6:30 a.m. The call was coming from a restricted number. I picked up, and it was Charlene on the other end, saying that she didn't appreciate how things were handled and that if she ever saw me again she was going to fuck me up. Sometimes people just can't leave well enough alone. I was done with the situation until she decided to pick up the phone and get it all started again. I was so upset, because I knew punk-ass Reese had given her my number, but that was okay, because I saw she still hadn't learned her lesson. I went to work that morning, and on the way, I called my girl Kali. I asked for her to get off of work early and meet me at her house so that she could take me to Charlene's. Charlene knew what my car looked like, so I had to be in another vehicle to be outside her apartment waiting for her to pull in from work. We waited for a few hours for her to come home.

Unfortunately, she didn't come through her front gate; she came in through her back gate. Her apartment faced the street where we were parked, and consequently, she spotted us while she was walking up the stairs to her place.

I got out of the car. "What's up now, Charlene?"

She must have bolted up those stairs to her apartment, because before I could get in the gate, she was in the house. I could see her looking from her window. I just got in the car and left, because somehow I knew she was going to call the police.

I was right. About two hours later, I received a call from the police asking if I knew her, and what had happened. How crazy! She started all this mess, and she lied and said I was outside stalking her. I told the police that she and I had a misunderstanding and that she wouldn't have to worry about me contacting her again. I was always getting the police called on me. Shame!

The next morning, the phone rang. I answered, "Hello?"

The voice on the other line said, "It's Reese."

"Why are you calling me? I have nothing to say to you."

He sighed. "Why would you go by Charlene's house and threaten her?"

"The same reason why she came over your house that night. No one is going to try and punk me and think I am okay with it!"

"Well, are you happy now? She says we aren't going to be friends anymore."

I chuckled. "I could care less! Get your punk ass off my line and don't hit me up ever again!"

It's funny how you can say something that you mean, but the other person somehow thinks that you didn't mean what you said. This was exactly what happened when Reese decided to contact me about two months later. He called asking if I could help him with some financial problems. He was behind in his mortgage payments and he was getting ready to lose his town-house. I'm sure his gambling addiction is the reason why he was behind on his payments, and the extra money that he was getting from Dre was not being spent on the mortgage payments.

I was taken a bit back for a moment that he had worked up the nerve to fix his mouth to ask such a thing. I told him, "Even if I could help you, I wouldn't." In my Erykah Badu voice, I sang, "You better call Charlene!" I hung up. I applauded myself for exhibiting some self-control with this situation, because previously, this could have turned really bad before I had a chance to process the whole thing.

Three years later, I ended up seeing him at the Magic Johnson 24 Hour Fitness. When he saw me, he waved. I waved back with my middle finger. He was acting like I was supposed to be happy to see him. I think not!

One day, I was walking out of the gym and he was walking in. He grabbed me and hugged me. I told him, "You got about two seconds to let me go before I grab your balls and twist them off!"

Reese let me go immediately. He had this astonished look on his face. I didn't care how much time had passed. He needed to know that he and I still weren't cool. From that day on, when he sees me, he looks and keeps going. I don't know what he was thinking, but after that ordeal, I was cool. After all, if you're not my friend, you're my enemy. There ain't no in-between with me!

Ealy – Didn't See That Coming

One day, I had a bright idea that I wanted to give back to the community by volunteering my time. I teamed up with a grassroots nonprofit organization that had no clue of what they were doing. They had no 501c number. How you going to have nonprofit as a part of your name when you don't even have your 501c number? Some of you may be thinking, what the hell is a 501c? It is a provision of the IRS exempting nonprofit organizations from federal income taxes. Since they didn't have that, it should have been the first clue to leave them the hell alone. Leave it up to me to ignore all the warning signs. Shame!

Clay was the founder, and Farrell was the flunky. I used to call Farrell the flunky only because he seemed to be riding Clay's coattail. I met with Clay and Farrell twice before they decided that it would be nice to have a giveaway of backpacks with school supplies. I thought it was a great idea until I learned they didn't have their 501c number and that they were planning on having this

event in less than two months. There was a way around
the 501c, which was to pair up with another established
nonprofit organization and use both names to promote
the event. However, they explained that Clay had previously spent his own money doing this event and that this
time they wanted sponsors to donate the backpacks and
supplies.

This would be a great idea if they weren't trying to
get sponsorship two months prior to the event. When
you put an event like this on, you have to ask for corporate sponsorships like almost a year of ahead of time. The
only time that you could put on something last minute
like that is when you already have an established relationship with the sponsors. They didn't. We teamed up
with a veteran NBA player who had a nonprofit organization. I was told to give his personal assistant/cousin
Ealy a call to get the ball rolling.

When I called Ealy, the phone conversation was very
short. He seemed in a rush and uninterested in helping
me. He stated that he would prefer to meet me in person
to discuss everything. He gave me an address where I
could meet him along with a time. I told him I would be
there.

We met at the NBA's player home. Over the phone,
Ealy had this strong Lou Rawls voice. I was anxious to
meet him to see what he looked like; it's always nice to
put a face with a voice. I normally don't mix business
with pleasure since that Mace incident, but since I was
volunteering my time, I figured there really wasn't any
harm.

I pulled up to a huge house that overlooked the Pacif-
ic Ocean. I got out of the car and made my way up ten
stairs. I rang the doorbell; it rang like chimes in a Catho-

lic church. When the door opened, there stood a man about 5'8", chocolate with a bald head. My first thought: *Yeah, this is just business.* I was totally unimpressed.

The house was all right, but nothing special for someone in the NBA. Don't get me wrong, it was a nice set up, but nothing jumped out at me and screamed that I was in a millionaire's house. Basically, it wouldn't have made it on MTV cribs. It was clean, nicely furnished, and huge. The player's trophies, MVP awards, pictures of him and fellow athletes in frames, and signed basketballs were the main decorations. There was truly a basketball shrine in his living room.

Ealy and I sat down. We began to talk about what the expectations, budgets, set up, location, guest list and costs of the event would be. After about an hour of discussion, we headed to the second level of the house to go work in the office on the computer.

Before entering into the office, he asked, "Would you like a tour of the house?"

In the back of mind, I was thinking, *Nope!* But I decided to be polite, so I said, "Sure!"

The second level had three bedrooms. One of them was the NBA player's hideaway; the other was the guest room. To my surprise, there was no office. The third room turned out to be Ealy's room.

I stood at the doorway and said, "You know, I have my laptop with me and I have some things saved on that, so let's work on that downstairs." He looked at me with hesitation in his eyes and I asked, "Okay?"

Before leaving the second level, he said he wanted to show me something. He took me up a winding flight of stairs. It was a third level that led to an outside patio with a fire pit and a beautiful view of the ocean. Out of all the things in the house, I must say I was finally impressed with this. I said, "This is nice!" and then I turned to walk down the stairs. I still wasn't impressed because this was not his house anyway.

We were finally done with drafting the sponsorship letter. Ealy asked, "Are you hungry?"

Since I love food, I said, "Yes."

I got my purse and we went down another level, which led to the garage. He turned on the light, and there sat an S-Class Mercedes and a Range Rover. He hit the car alarm and the headlights of the truck came on. He opened my door for me, then he got in and asked, "Where would you like to go?"

"It doesn't matter."

We went to California Pizza Kitchen to grab something to eat. During our meal, he asked, "What are you doing for the weekend?"

"Why?"

He smiled. "Because I would like to take you with me to Miami."

I think I may have choked on my food. "Miami! What's in Miami?"

He explained, "Alonzo Mourning is having some type of three-day weekend charity event."

Everything within me wanted to say yes, what time should I be there, what time do we leave, when we coming back, what should I wear? Instead, I said, "No, I already have plans, but thanks anyways."

He seemed stunned. See, men like Ealy expect for women to be all over them just because he has or is associated with money. I wasn't impressed with Ealy. He wasn't the NBA player, he was the personal assistant. Plus, with a trip to Miami, I'm sure there would have been some strings attached. There would have been more involved than me just being his date for the weekend. Plus, I was getting ready to have surgery on my foot that Monday, and that was more important than some weekend getaway.

Ealy stayed in two places to live, but while he was out of town, he would correspond via phone, text, and email with me. Eventually, his frumpy lil self began to grow on me, and that was so not part of the plan. I explained to him that whatever we were about to start up, it would be best that it wait until after the event.

Even though I had foot surgery, I was still willing to make the event happen. However, a week before the event, the goal for sponsorship hadn't been met. We did have donations that could still be of use. However, Clay and Farrell insisted that the supplies that we had were not enough to provide to 500 children. So instead of giving out what we had to the children, those two idiots decided to cancel the event altogether.

I was dazed by their decision. I just couldn't believe that they would call me the day before the event to tell me that we were cancelling the event. I was so ashamed to call some of the sponsors and the media to tell them that the event would not be taking place. I was hotter than fish grease, because my name was associated with this ghetto-hot mess. After that day, I parted ways with Clay and Farrell.

I may have parted ways with the people that were responsible for me meeting Ealy, but I didn't part ways with Ealy. He and I begin to date. We went everywhere. When I say everywhere, I mean everywhere! We went shopping and we ate at the most prestigious places. He was spending money like he had a money tree in his backyard. I thought to myself, *This lifestyle ain't too bad for a personal assistant.* All this pampering treatment ended after six weeks. It was time for him to go back to another state to handle some business. Being out with him was like being Cinderella. Don't get me wrong, I had my own money, car, place, etc., but it wasn't on that luxury level. I had gotten a taste of the good life once again, and I wanted more.

Ealy made multiple calls to me while he was out of town. He would say how much he missed me, and how he couldn't wait to see me. He stated that he wanted me to move closer, like to a beach property, so that when he came into town, I could be more accessible. He offered to move me into a townhouse. I would be lying if I said he didn't pique my curiosity. However, I just couldn't allow him to have that much control over me. Before we got off the phone, he stated that he wanted to spend some time with me away from LA, and that he would like to take me to Santa Barbara for the weekend. I said sure.

I was so excited to be going on a little getaway! I packed my cutest, sexiest outfits in my Louis Vuitton bags. I picked Ealy up from the airport, but we didn't leave that same night to go to Santa Barbara. Instead, we spent the night at the house. I thought it was time that I rewarded Ealy for being so nice. I gave him some of my cookies, and he liked it. He liked it so much that we did it about a few times. He was pretty decent in bed, except there was one setback. He wanted me to give him head. Don't get me wrong, there is nothing wrong with a little head. But not just anyone gets oral sex from me. He was real aggressive in trying to get me to do it. He must not have gotten the memo: I only do what I want to do.

The next morning we woke, showered, dressed, and went to breakfast at Jerry's Deli. I thought that his choice to go to Jerry's was a bit odd since we usually ate at nicer places. I just went with the flow. The whole time during breakfast, he handled business calls, barely speaking to me. Again, I found this unusual, as he normally liked to run his mouth. I just shrugged it off and ate my meal.

The ride back to the house was silent. When we arrived back at the house, we went into the kitchen, and I began to ask when we were leaving for the trip.

Ealy said, "Ooh, I forgot to tell you I have a business meeting at 1:00 p.m."

I asked, "How long is that going to last?"

"Not that long."

"Am I going with you?"

"No. You can stay here and wait for me."

I said, "What if I want to leave and come back?"

He replied, "I'm setting the alarm, so that isn't an option. Or you can go shopping if you want." He then pulled out $300. I took the shopping.

He sent me a few texts throughout the day because his meeting went past the time he said he would be done. When he finally called, I was out to dinner with my girl Neena. He said, "I'm going to have to pass on the trip." I was disappointed. "The business discussed in the meeting ended up with some things having to be handled immediately," he went on to explain. "You can come get your luggage that is at the house."

When I arrived at the house, there was no sign of Ealy. I wanted to wait for him, however, the neighborhood was upper class and I didn't need anyone calling the police saying that I was in front of the NBA player's house stalking him. I got on the freeway, and while driving home, I made several phone calls to Ealy, which all went unanswered. I left a few messages and sent a few texts. At that point, I was becoming more upset, since I had to leave without my luggage. Keyword: *my* luggage, which I purchased prior to even meeting him.

Two days went by and I still hadn't heard from him, yet he still had my belongings in his possession. I called, emailed, and texted, all with no reply. I drove back down to LA, determined to get my belongings.

He must have sensed the wrath coming, because all of a sudden I received a phone call from him. Ealy said, "Come get your stuff from the house."

Thirty minutes later, I received another call with him giving me another address to meet him at. I arrived at that address, and still no sign of Ealy. I sat there for almost an hour. Again, I started to text and call him; still no answer. I had Taylor call him from her work phone, and he answered when she called. I had my Aunt Tonya call from her cell phone, and he answered her call as well. When he answered, she told him he needed to give me back my stuff, and he hung up on her. It was clear that he was taking everyone else's calls but mine.

Forty-five minutes later, I received a call from Ealy. He said, "Meet me at the house."

While I was en route to the house, he called and said he couldn't make it. At this, point I was outraged by his tactics. I finally just said, "Forget it!"

I went over to Kali's house. I could always go to her house to wait out traffic. So, I was chilling with her and watching a movie when I got a call. It was Ealy, telling me to come to the house. Kali and I got in the car and made our way over there. When I arrived, there was a Hyundai parked in front of the house.

She asked, "Do you want me to go to the door with you?"

I turned to Kali and said, "Stay in the car."

If you haven't realized it by now, Kali was my ride-or-die homegirl, and she was ready to set it off at any moment. As I got out of the car to go to the steps, I looked up and saw the fire pit going with the giggles of a woman and Ealy's voice coming from the third floor. I looked up, and there he was getting cozy with someone else. I was broken-hearted. This is when I realized I had just gotten played by the personal assistant. All his ass wanted was some ass. Once he got it, he was done with me. This was nothing unusual for a man to do to a woman. But he was like so cold with it, the *bam* right in your face, was just blatantly wrong. It was almost as wrong as Mashon showing up on my front doorstep with his new girlfriend.

The icing on the cake wasn't quite finished yet. As I walked to the door, there were my two bags of luggage sitting on the front porch. Ooh, my God! I began to ring that doorbell—like Beyoncé says, ring the alarm. I started ringing that damn bell like the house next door was on fire. It's not like I didn't know he wasn't home, because I could see he was on the balcony. Finally, after I didn't get an answer, I just dropped my head, picked up my stuff, and got in the car. To make matters worse, I heard the girl call me a dumb bitch as I was walking to my car. I thought, *You have no idea who the fuck you are messing with!*

When I got in the car, Kali asked, "What the fuck just happened?"

I lowered my head. "I have been played."

Kali lived about twenty minutes from there, so we went back to her house. I could have easily have just

walked away, since I had my luggage back in my possession. But that just wasn't good enough. I was enraged
that this lil man was treating me like a groupie girl when
he wasn't even the NBA player; he was the damn personal assistant! Man, is you serious!

Kali and I arrived at her house. She said, "What are
you going to do?" She knew me well enough to know
that I wasn't going to let him get a pass for his actions.

I said, "Give me one of your sweat suits." I put the
sweat suit over my clothes. I told her to give me a pair of
her tennis shoes too.

She side-eyed me. "What?"

I repeated, "Some tennis shoes!"

"What about your foot?" Kali asked.

I had been wearing a foot brace the whole time due to
the surgery. Kali gave me a confused look. "You sure you
want tennis shoes? You're not supposed to be wearing a
shoe yet."

I said, "I will be just fine. What I got in mind will only
take a second."

Kali was about three inches taller than me, which
made her sweat suit a perfect fit. It was baggy, just like I
needed it to be.

We waited for about another hour before we headed
back out to go pay Ealy a visit. I circled his street one
time, waited twenty minutes, then circled again. There
was no sign of the two lovebirds on the balcony. I parked
the car around the corner. I took off my foot brace and
forced the tennis shoe on my foot. I took the hood of the
sweat jacket and placed it over my head. I then popped
my trunk where I kept a knife at all times. This was a
handy tool. It cuts through rubber like it was hot bread

and butter. Kali had been on so many capers with me that she already knew what her role was.

I started off limping down the street, but once I got to his street, I straightened my walk as much as possible. I knew that there were cameras on the house. One was at the corner of the garage, another on the porch, and the other was almost on the roof. I held my head down so that the hood draped over the top of my head. I approached the car parked on the street and slashed all four tires on the vehicle parked out front. I proceeded to pick up a decorative rock on the grass. I threw the rock in an attempt to shatter the garage door. The rock was super heavy, which made my aim off. It hit the house instead, causing a large thump. I looked up, and I didn't think anyone saw me, but I took off running anyway. I couldn't believe that I had done all this on an injured foot.

Kali was waiting for me at the top of the corner of the next street. When she saw me coming, she jumped in the passenger side and started the car. I hopped in the car, took off, dropped her off, then headed home.

When I got home, I turned the ringer off on my phone. I needed rest from the last two days. It had turned out to be mentally and physically exhausting to me. I fell asleep. I woke up probably around 11:00 a.m. When I picked up the cell phone, I had ten missed calls. From who? Who else but Ealy! He sent me a text saying that I was going to jail, that I was on video, that I slashed the tires of an off-duty police officer car, and that I was going to have to pay for the car being towed and the new tires. He was just going on and on.

My confidence was never shaken since I have heard threats before, and this would be the hundredth time someone called the police on me. I picked up the phone and called him. I said, "How can I help you?"

The first thing he said was, "The police are looking for you."

I guess you might be wondering why they didn't just come to my house and question me. My number one rule was to never, ever show any man where I lived. There was no reason for them to know of my residency unless we had been seeing each other longer than three months. Unfortunately, many never made it past two months before they decided to show their asses. Anyways, I knew he was lying, because if the police were going to question me, they would have run my name through the system to get my address. Then I would have been having a conversation with them instead of him.

I told him, "Look, I don't know what you are talking about."

Ealy said, "I saw your car on tape, then your friend slashed the tires!" I could tell he had no clue that the "friend" was me.

I chuckled. "Did you see a car *like* mine or my car, because there is a difference."

"You can try to be slick all you want, but I know it was you!" Ealy retorted. "The police are coming to your house and arresting you!"

Once again, there is a difference between knowing and proving. The mere fact that he had someone on video slashing tires and didn't know it was me ended that conversation. "I'm sorry, I have no idea what you are talking about," I said calmly. "I was nowhere near there last night. After you dumped my bags on the porch, I went home. Too bad that happened. You should be more selective with who you allow to come to your boss's home!" I hung up. The police never showed up at my house that day, or any other day for that matter. He was simply lying trying to get me to confess.

I was really trying to change, but one part of me just couldn't die so easily. I really wanted to let Ealy get away with the fact that he had played me, but I just couldn't. I had to show this man that no matter who you are, who you work for, where you live, or how much money you got it is never ok to try to dog Kennedee Devoe. I have always believed in karma, but the only thing about karma is that usually you're nowhere around to see the justice served. This had become my mentality since I was a young girl in the beginning stages of dating. It carried over into adulthood and became more aggressive with each cheating and lying man.

You would think that after all that happened, Ealy would have just gone his separate way. His crazy butt called about a month later, apologizing for his actions. However, I needed for him to provide an explanation for why he did me the way he did. He had no answer, and seemed clueless as to what I was talking about. The incident that took place was something that neither of us saw coming, and we both definitely underestimated each other's capabilities. No matter the apology, my point was made, and there was no reason for us to have any further contact. There was nothing more that could be said or done.

Braxton – An Ass Whippin' Will Change Your Life

After that crazy incident with Ealy, I decided that I would give dating a break for a moment. However, a moment for me tends to not last very long. When you're single and wanting a man in your life, waiting can seem like an eternity. It was the summer of 2006, and I hadn't been dating for the last twelve months. I was on a late-night run to Los Angeles when I came upon a 7-Eleven store. I went in to grab a delicious Slurpee.

As I was walking to my car, someone began to flash their bright lights on me. When I looked to see who it was, there was a guy sitting in a Chrysler 300M with the mesh-style grill (aka Bentley grill), tinted windows, and 22 inch rims. I didn't recognize the car, so I proceeded to get into my own car, but the bright lights flashed from the car again. This time, the driver motioned for me to come to the car. I don't walk to cars. If you want me, you must put in the work. So I motioned for him to drive over.

When he pulled up to the car, there awaited a dark-skinned guy with chiseled features. He said, "Girl, what's a pretty girl like you doing out here in the middle of the night?"

I fired back with, "What are you doing hanging out in a parking lot pimping in the middle of the night?"

He laughed. "I'm waiting for my homeboy to meet me so we can go to the club."

"Well, I was just stopping to quench my thirst."

He looked me up and down. "Do you want to go with me to La Louisiana?"

I shook my head. "No, I have some running around to do."

"Where do you live?"

I answered, "In San Dimas."

"Ohhh, really? I stay about twenty minutes from there."

"Yes, really!"

"Maybe we can hook up and do something some-time?"

His name was Braxton, and I did end up calling and taking him up on his offer, however, he was hard to get in touch with. We played phone tag for about two weeks until we finally made definite plans. I said I would come over to his house and cook dinner for him. When I got there, I wasn't very impressed with the outside of the house, but when I entered the house itself, I must say this man had excellent decorating taste for a man. From the living room to the bathroom to the kitchen to the bed-room, every room was decorated with contemporary designs. He had a beautiful indigo-blue pool out back. The tour finished off in the kitchen, where I found every appliance known to man. I was definitely impressed with the kitchen arrangement, because most men that have bachelor pads tend to have only the bare necessities there.

We went to the store to get what we needed to make dinner. I thought about grilling some salmon or shrimp, but he insisted that we have chicken. I told him, "I don't eat fried chicken nor do I fix it."

Braxton asked, "Well, how do you fix it?"

I replied, "Either I grill, bake, or steam it."

"I'd prefer it if you bake it."

So we got the chicken, seasonings, cauliflower, and potatoes to bake. I was very impressed with the kitchen, because he had a 15-inch flat screen in the kitchen equipped with cable. It was great! I could watch TV and cook at the same time. I made baked chicken, steamed veggies, and mashed potatoes.

I brought his plate into the dining room. Braxton licked his lips and said, "This looks good."

"Thanks!"

Braxton got up from the table, went into the kitchen, and came back with a bottle of ketchup. He then began to pour the ketchup on his chicken as well as his potatoes. I was totally grossed out. That was the most ghetto thing I had seen in a while. I felt a little upset, because before he could even taste the food to see if he liked it, he started pouring ketchup all over it. I mean, who pours ketchup all over their food? Well, I know I don't! Anyone that knows me knows that I am no fan of condiments. So I guess that's why I was turned off. In my mind, I thought this man was not on the same level as me. That would be like going to Lawry's and pouring ketchup all over the steak. Funny how lil things can be a deal breaker. I did not have much conversation with him after that.

I cleaned the kitchen when I was done and he walked me out to the car. He tried to kiss me on the lips, but I said, "You can give me a kiss on the cheek." I didn't want his ketchup lips on me…ugh!

As I drove home, I thought, *What a waste of time.* I was just irritated by him pouring that damn ketchup on his food. It's funny how something so small can turn you off about a person. I made up my mind that night that he and I wouldn't be talking after that night.

About a week went by, and I figured he had gotten the picture, since I hadn't called since that night. I guess I was wrong. He called a few times, but I didn't answer. He would leave messages offering dinner and outings. I wasn't swayed by his attempts at first.

Braxton called one night from a blocked number. He must have figured that was the only way that I would answer. He asked, "Is there something I did? You haven't called me."

I told him, "I just don't think that we are compatible."

"Can you give me a chance to prove you wrong?"

I thought, *This could be interesting,* so I said yes.

He started off by taking me to some nice restaurants like Stinky Rose, Morton's, and Lawry's. I was impressed. Since he had poured ketchup all over his chicken, I was surprised that he had that kind of taste in food, and he didn't pour ketchup all over any of these meals. Thank goodness!

We never really did any recreational activities, just mostly dinner. So when he asked for me to take a ride on his Harley with him, I was excited. I had never ridden on a motorcycle before, because I was always afraid that I would get hurt on one. However, I was trying to show that I could be a trooper, so I agreed.

I headed over to his house. He was already outside wiping his bike down. It was a deep purple color with bluish undertones. I asked, "Where are we going?"

"Shopping."

"For who?"

"For us," he said with a smile.

I was with that, because I love to shop. He handed me a helmet and helped me get it on. He revved up the bike, and we took off with the radio he had in his motorcycle bumping Too Short's "Blow the Whistle". We headed towards the 210 freeway. However, the mall was the opposite way. I thought maybe we were taking the long way to the mall.

Once we got on the freeway, instead of going south we went north. I began to worry about where the hell we were going. I yelled, "I thought we were going to the mall?"

He yelled back, "I told you were going shopping. I never said where."

There we were on the freeway, looking like we were headed to Las Vegas. Thank God we only ended up in Barstow! When he finally parked that bike, I was so glad to get off. My ass, thighs, and back were killing me. This man had taken me on an hour and a half motorcycle ride to go to the damn outlet stores all the way in freaking Barstow. I was madder than mad, but I tried to play it off.

He kept his word, and we went shopping. However, since we were on a bike, our purchases were limited. Braxton brought me some designer sunglasses, perfume, and a pair of Nikes. He bought himself just a pair of shoes. We stayed and ate a meal, and then it was back on the motorcycle for the ride home. I thought that the ride up there was bad...but man, we hit so much traffic coming back that it took us almost two hours to get back to his house. I couldn't even play it off when we got back, my body was so sore.

He asked, "Can I draw you a bath?"

I said, "Please do!"

I finally got into a tub full of hot water with bubbles and just soaked my poor little body. When I was done, he came and helped me out of the tub. He took me to the bed and laid me down. He started to pour lotion all over me, and he rubbed it deeply into my skin. He started to give me a deep tissue massage, and it felt so right. He got me all relaxed; I ended up just falling asleep.

The more time we spent together, the more time I realized what a gentleman Braxton was. For me, it has always been the small things that count to me. One day, he saw that my car had a flat. Unlike Royce, who tried to make me change the tire myself, Braxton didn't even call AAA; he got on his hands and knees and changed it for me. That really meant a lot to me. A few days later, he pointed out that another tire was going bad, and he said, "I will just purchase a whole new set of tires. Be here tomorrow morning and we will go and get you the tires."

The next morning I showed up per his request. However, as I pulled up to the house, I noticed that an unidentified car was parked in front. I didn't think too much of it because he had told me to come back over there that morning. I rang the doorbell, but there was no answer. I rang it again, and still no answer. I called him from my cell phone, not once, but twice. I rang the doorbell one last time, and he finally came to the door.

He opened the door halfway with his body in the doorframe. I said, "What, you didn't hear me? Were you sleeping or something?"

He said, "Something like that."

"Are you going to let me in?" As soon as I asked that question, I heard a woman coughing. I frowned. "So you got someone up in here? Is this the reason why you took so long to answer the door or your phone?"

"Don't trip!"

"What do you mean 'don't trip'?"

Braxton said, "Let me put some clothes on," and then he closed the door.

I started to walk to my car, because no matter what he had to say, it wasn't going to make a world of a difference at that point. I was almost to the car when I heard his garage door coming up. I looked back, and he was walking out his garage door with some chicken-head girl. This chick was so ghetto it looked like he had gone to the heart of the ghetto and picked her up. She had burgundy and black braids in her hair, she was smoking a cigarette from a pack of Kool's, and she had super-long acrylic nails with jewels and designs on them. She looked like the type of hood chick that would be dramatic and would fight at a drop of a dime, for any small reason. Later on, I would find that I was right.

I asked Braxton, "Who is that?"

She rolled her eyes. "Don't worry about it, because I already know who you are, and I know about you."

I tried to maintain my calmness by being a well-spoken and well-mannered woman so she would know that she wasn't dealing with a fellow hood chick. I said, "Do you mind going back inside so that he and I can discuss this matter together?"

She shot back, "I ain't going nowhere, bitch!

I looked at him and said, "Could you please ask your friend to go back inside so that we can talk alone?"

Braxton turned to the girl. "Can you go back in the house?"

But she still stood there in the garage like she didn't hear a thing he said. I asked him, "How does she know about me?"

He shrugged. "Because I told her."

"And why would you do that?"

"She asked if I had a girl and I didn't want to lie."

"So it's okay to tell her about me, yet I am clueless as to who she is?"

She said, "Bitch, you don't need to worry about who I am!"

By this time, her mouthiness was beginning to get on my nerves. I think that I had given her the wrong impression that I was scared of her when all I was trying to do was keep the situation calm. I finally had to stand up for myself to let her know that even though I was attractive and classy, it didn't mean I wouldn't get in her ass.

I said, "Who the fuck you keep calling a bitch? You the motherfucking bitch up here, laying up with someone else's man! You think it's cute or okay just because you know about me? Don't get it twisted, bitch I will come up there and whip your ass! You look like shit, bitch! Go in the house with your ugly ass." I must have hit a nerve because she started walking out of the garage. As she started approaching me, I said, "What the fuck you think that you about to do?"

At this point, Braxton started walking toward her. "Take your ass in the house!" He turned to me and said,

"Please be quiet. You know I live in a white neighbor-hood."

"So what? You should have thought about that before you brought this trash over here!" I retorted.

He pleaded, "Come on, Kennedee, you gotta keep it down before they call the police!"

"Good! They will be here in enough time to witness the beat down, because if she steps another foot towards me, it's going to be on!"

This chick kept telling Braxton, "Let her go, let her go!"

I taunted, "Yeah, let her go so she can get her ass whipped for talking all that shit about me!" I turned to her. "You don't know me, chick! Don't let the face fool you! I will get in that ass!"

She said, "Well, bring it then!" She finally went back in the house, then she came right back out. She headed for her car and grabbed her overnight bag from the trunk. She turned towards my car and took a picture of my license plate with her camera phone.

I scoffed, "What, am I supposed to be scared or some-thing?"

She laughed. "I will see you around soon, bitch, and you better not be slipping!"

"Well, let's handle it now!" She ignored me, walked in the house, and never came back. I told him, "I am so done with you! You're going to have that trash over here and have her talking to me disrespectfully, and you don't say a word? You're a sorry ass man!"

He tried to explain, but if you heard one lie, you have heard them all. I didn't have time for a repeat script with a different character. I just got in the car and left.

Days later, I walked outside to my car to find my tires slashed. I can only assume that it was that trashy whore that I had the altercation with. I immediately called Braxton and told him what happened. He said that I was bullshitting and hung up on me. I was so upset that this loser thought that I was trying to make up an excuse to see him or talk to him and get my new tires. I had to replace the tires myself, but I thought, *Someone is going to have to pay.* I didn't know how to find the girl, but I sure knew how to find Braxton. It seemed logical at the time, since my tires wouldn't have been slashed if it wasn't for dealing with him. I thought maybe he should experience the same thing.

He belonged to a motorcycle club, and he had discussed with me a few weeks prior that he was going on the Fresno run with this club. I knew that he wouldn't be taking any of his cars with him, so that would be the perfect opportunity.

That Friday night, the bikers were set to leave. I went out to dinner with Taylor and Erin in Hollywood at Memphis. The food was delicious, and the atmosphere was relaxing. We had a good time, and by the time we were finished eating, it was 12:30 a.m. After dinner, I decided that would be the best time to drive over to his house.

When I finally got to his house, it was about two o'clock in the morning. I parked my car a block away and walked up the street with the rubber cutter in my hand. He had left both of his cars parked in the driveway. The first set of tires I slashed was his 22's on his 300M. Next I slashed the Mercedes Benz R-Class. I am not quite sure what size the tires were on the Mercedes, but I can remember that they had nice rims on them, and the car was only a few months old. I walked quickly to my car, got in, and took off.

That Sunday evening, Braxton was due back from his Fresno trip, but I knew he wouldn't be going straight home. I was in LA that night because my girl Tina had just given birth to her first son. I was coming out of the hospital from visiting her when I got a call on my cell phone.

It was Braxton. He asked, "Are you in LA."

"Why?" I retorted.

He answered, "Because I want you to come down to the motorcycle club to come get the money for the tires. I feel bad that the girl did that to your car."

"I'm on my way."

It was crowded at the party. I couldn't find a parking spot in front of or near the building. I drove down the side street to park; however, it was way too dark for my taste. So instead, I pulled up to the corner of the place, parked in the red, and called him from my cell phone.

Braxton said, "Come inside!"

From the looks of the crowd, that didn't seem like a good idea. "No, I don't think so."

He said, "Okay, I will be right out." As he walked to the car, I unlocked the door.

He got in the car and said, "What's up?"

I said, "You tell me!"

"You know that shit you pulled wasn't cool, right?"

"No, what *she* pulled wasn't okay!"

Braxton frowned. "You know what I am talking about! Did you think that you were going to get away with that shit?"

As I sat there astonished, it clicked that he knew his tires were slashed. I saw two teenage girls approaching the car. It was more like they bum-rushed the car, because they were walking aggressively to the car. At that very moment, I realized I had been set up. He had lured me down here, pretending not to have a clue about what happened, in order for these girls to kill, fight, beat or jump me.

As the two girls approached the car, I turned to him and said, "Look, it don't have to go down like this."

Braxton chuckled. "You should have thought about that before you did what you did! He took my keys out of the ignition and threw them out the window. I kept a spare key in the glove compartment. I reached over to get it out of this mini wallet I kept it in. I got it and had it in my hands, but he grabbed it and threw it in the back seat.

By this time, the girls were at my driver's side door. He reached around me and popped the lock up. I hurried and slammed it back down. He reached around me again. This time he used both hands, one to pop the lock and the other to open the door handle. Once the door handle was released, he pushed out so the door could open. He jumped out of the passenger's door, and that was the girls' cue that they had me.

I pulled the door closed and held it with all my might. However, with both of them pulling at the top of the door, they definitely had the upper hand on me. I couldn't let that door loose, because I knew what waited for me: the ass whipping of my life! It would have been different if it was one girl, but two? That's a different story. One of them finally pulled the door open. I could feel one girl's hand wrap around my long ponytail and yank me out of the car by it. From there on, everything just seemed to happen so fast.

The one who pulled me out by hair had now grabbed the ponytail holder off my hair and shook my hair all over my head. I couldn't see a damn thing. It was like fighting in the dark. They begin to administer fist blows. One was hitting me from the front and the other from the back. When I finally got a feeling as to both of their positions, I was able to defend myself. My plan was to finish off the one in front first then deal with the one behind me. I was able to grab hold of the hair of the girl that was in front of me. Once I got a hold of her, I started to just hit her over and over again in the face. I wouldn't stop delivering the blows to her face.

In the midst of the fight, I heard one of them yell, "Get that bitch's earrings!"

I had on diamond earrings that night, and let's just say that after that fight, they had to be replaced. My plan for defense and survival was working until the one from behind me reached around and attempted to punch me. Her hit made contact with my right eye, and immediately, I started to bleed. As the warm blood hit my face, I became startled, causing me to lose focus in the fight. That very second I lost momentum, she was able to gain the upper hand by grabbing me and throwing me to down to the ground.

The two girls were now in control of this fight, because as soon as I was on the ground, one of them started to kick me in the head. That lasted for only thirty seconds... thank God! They only stopped because of the oncoming traffic that started to come down the street. The traffic from the main street saw us in the middle of the street and began to honk. Someone yelled, "Get off of her! I am going to call the police."

The oncoming traffic was the only thing that saved me. They began to flee the scene on foot. Even though the people in the cars were honking and screaming, no one ever stopped to help. How crazy is that? I got up staggering to my car. I felt something warm and wet somewhere on my face. When I touched my eyebrow to see what it was, I brought my hand down to look, and it was a whole lot of blood.

I began to panic and check my surroundings to be sure that they were gone. When I looked to my left, it looked as if all the people from the party were outside to see me get my ass whipped. When I got into my car, I hurried and pulled the driver's side mirror down to see what my face looked like. I know it sounds vain, but I had to see what damage they had done to me. I looked in the mirror, and surprisingly, the only damage was a small cut over my eye that was bleeding profusely. I put the mirror back up and reached for the keys to start the car, but there were no keys because he had tossed them out the window. I reached in the back seat to get the mini wallet with the spare, but the key wasn't in there. I really began to panic, because I needed to get out of there, and I wasn't sure if he had picked up the keys once he got out of the car.

I was sitting there when two guys walked by the car. I can't front; I was scared, because I thought they were there to finish the job. They came to the passenger's side window, and one of them said, "Baby girl, you need to get out of here!"

"I know, but I can't leave because I don't have my keys. He threw them out the window."

The two guys looked around, found them, and handed them to me. The one guy said, "Now you should leave."

I said, "Okay," and they walked off.

I went to put the key in the ignition, but it wasn't going in. I took a look at the keys, and the key was broken. He had pulled the key so hard when he took it out that he had broken the other half in the ignition. I hurried up, jumped out of the car, and began to walk down the street with blood streaming from my face.

As I was walking down the street, I saw a bum looking at me. As I approached him, he picked up the receiver on the pay phone next to him, pretending like he didn't see me so he wouldn't have to help me. Even though I was hurt, I was appalled that a bum of all people had the nerve to act as if he couldn't help me.

I had my cell phone on me, but I used a pay phone to call 911 so that they could pinpoint a location for me. The 911 operator asked what my emergency was. I told them that I had just been jumped by two girls. The operator asked for my name, what I had on, and what happened. She told me to stay on the line while the fire department came. I said, "The fire department? I need the police."

She explained, "They are both being dispatched to the scene. Stay on the line until they get there."

There was a McDonald's on the corner where I was calling from. The employees that worked there saw me bleeding, and one of them came out and brought me a handful of napkins. The employee asked, "Are you okay? Do you need anything else?"

I shook my head. "Thanks, but the police are already on their way. I appreciate you coming out and checking on me."

The employee went back inside, and the rest of the restaurant crew continued to watch out for me through the drive-thru window until the fire department showed up.

I was so upset that the fire department had arrived before the police department did! The fire truck pulled up to the corner, and about eight firefighters jumped out of the truck. They began to check me to make sure I was okay. I thought that I only had a nick on my eye, but there was blood coming through my right pant leg, and my left elbow was hurt too. They gave me a cold pack to apply to my eye to stop the bleeding. They told me that I needed to go to the hospital to get stitches for the cut over my eye.

I explained, "I don't want to leave my car there! The key is broken off in the ignition, the car won't start, and the passenger side window is down." I knew if I left my car there that night, I would not have a car to pick up the next morning.

One of the firemen was very nice. He went to look at the car and came back and said, "Did you know that your car was still on?"

I said, "It was?"

"Yes, it was. Come back to the car with me so that I can show you how to turn the car on and off."

When we got to the car, he explained, "You take the broken piece and align it with the broken piece inside the ignition to start the car."

"Thank you so much!" I said gratefully. "I appreciate your help!"

Finally, the police arrived. The officers began to ask me what happened.

I told them, "This guy set me up and had some girls jump and rob me." Right then, I remembered the girls saying to each other to get my earrings. I began to touch my ears, and that's when I realized that my diamond earrings were gone. I touched my neck, and my chain was missing. Nasir had bought me a diamond-encrusted platinum chain with the initial K. Well, that was gone too. I was in disbelief that all of this was happening to me while I had been waiting for the police to arrive.

I used my cell phone to call my cousin Derwin while on the phone with 911. He showed up while the police were questioning me, and just the look on his face was one of concern. I had never seen Derwin look like that before. He looked like he wanted to break down and cry. His eyes filled with tears. All I could do was give him a hug, because I felt his emotions. I just started crying uncontrollably in his arms.

The officer asked me, "Can you gather your composure so that you can make a statement? We need a description of the people who did this to you."

"The girls were between the ages of sixteen and eighteen. They were probably about 5'5" but no more than 5'6", and both of them weighed probably between 120-135 pounds."

The officer asked, "Can you tell me what they were wearing?"

"It happened so fast, I'm glad I could even remember that much."

"Are you sure it was two girls?"

I said, "Yes, why?"

"You don't look like you were jumped. I have seen people that were involved in a one person fight, and they looked worse than you. You must have really held your own."

I shrugged. "I had no choice. If I hadn't fought back, I probably would be dead right now."

"What's a girl like you doing on this side of town anyway?"

I replied, "My ex-boyfriend asked me to come down to talk with me, but he set me up." I didn't dare tell him that I had slashed this man's tires and he was trying to have me killed over it.

The officer went on to ask me for Braxton's address and telephone number, but I told them that he was right there at that party - they should go in and arrest him. Why did the officers look at me like I was crazy? How are you going to be a police officer and be scared? Unbelievable!

"You want us to go into the party and arrest him?" one officer said doubtfully.

"That's correct."

They said, "We would have to call for backup, and probably by the time they get here, he will be gone."

Derwin pulled me to the side and said, "What the hell, are you crazy? You can't have them go in there and look for him! You will cause a riot!"

"Fine!" I huffed. But I knew that the only way that they were going to catch him was right then and there.

The officers finished up the report and said that Braxton and the girls would be charged with assault and robbery. They gave me a police report number and their business card with their names and numbers. They watched as I got into my car to make sure that we drove off safely.

My cousin was parked on a different side of the street. I drove him to his car. I had him follow me to Mallory's house. When I knocked on the door, her boyfriend answered and let me in.

Mallory was so mad at me for going down to see Braxton by myself! All she could do was sit there and shake her head. "He needs to get his ass whipped for this!" Mallory's boyfriend Danny began to administer first aid again on me. The cut above my eye had begun to bleed again. He cleaned the cut with peroxide and put Neosporin and a fresh Band-Aid on it. All I could do was cry because I had gotten myself into this situation. If only I hadn't let my anger get the best of me for the thousandth time.

We all went outside, where my cousin was still waiting for me. They all began to talk about the incident and how messed up it was that Braxton had retaliated like that. But to be honest, he had the right. I never should have done what I did to him, but damn, I didn't think he would come back like that!

By this time, Jackson and I were back on speaking terms. I called him on my way home, and he kept me company. He was frantic and concerned about me. I was honestly good until I spoke with him, but he just heightened the whole situation, which put me on the edge.

Jackson kept asking, "Are you going to be okay? Are you sure he doesn't know where you live?" He kept on and on with "what if this happens", "what if that happens". He really didn't help the situation much.

When I got to my house, it was almost 4:00 in the morning. I was low-key paranoid, because I had not planned on being gone for that long, and all the lights were out. I was scared walking into a dark house, because I wasn't sure what waited for me.

When I got in the house, I turned on every light in the house. I walked into my bedroom and begin to take my clothes off. I had forgotten that my knee and elbow were injured. When I felt them both, they had started bleeding again. My clothing had scratched off the bandages. I went into the bathroom to get Band-Aids. I opened the medicine cabinet. As I closed the door, I caught I glimpse of myself in the mirror. I looked like hell. I wasn't severely hurt, but a piece of me was stolen away that night.

The next morning when I woke up, I was stiff as a brick. My body was sore all over, and it felt like I had just gone twelve rounds with Laila Ali. My eye with the small cut had swollen a smidge. I just got some ice and laid down for the rest of the day.

As the word began to spread in my circle, everyone called to check on me. Later on that evening, the police called. They said they needed me to come down so that they could get pictures of my injuries for the case. I told them that I would be down the following day.

A few hours later, I received a phone call from Braxton. He had called from a blocked number. "The police are calling me and questioning me about what happened last night. Why did you call the police?"

I said, "How dare you even call this number?" You think you have the right to question me about anything after what you did?"

"You were wrong too for slashing my tires! Do you know how much it's going to cost to replace the tires?"

I shouted, "Are you serious, are you fucking serious? You are sitting there worried about replacing tires? Do you know what could have happened to me if that fight would have gotten out of hand? You can go out and replace a set of tires. If I would have been killed, my mother would not have been able to go out and replace me with another Kennedee. Now you can get the fuck off of my phone!" I hung up. I was so disgusted with myself and with him all this behind some bullshit-ass tires, and a situation that I could have easily walked away from if I had not let my appetite for vengeance get the best of me.

The next morning, I received a phone call from Braxton's cousin Charles. He said, "I'm sorry to hear about what happened. Could you cease retaliation against Braxton or any members of his family?"

I asked him, "Now why would you call with a request like that?"

He said, "I'm very aware of who your family is."

"Who is my family?"

He stated, " I know your cousin DJ." DJ was a triple, triple OG from a well-known gang in LA.

I told him, "I have to go; don't call me again." Truth be told, I had no idea of pursuing this situation with street justice or with the legal system. I just really wanted this whole incident to go away.

When I went to the police station, they took pictures of me and told me that they should be arresting Braxton shortly. I don't know what shortly was. Two weeks later, I called in to check on the status of the case.

The officer told me that he had spoken with Braxton's lawyer, and they were supposed to be coming down to the station. The officer asked, "How did you get involved with a guy like Braxton?"

"What do you mean?"

He stated that Braxton was on his third strike with this charge. He informed me that he had previously been arrested on gun-related charges, but couldn't tell me what they were, and that he was also affiliated with a gang on the eastside of LA. I was in disbelief that this guy had a record and was gang-related. At that point, I knew I had to call my big cousin.

I called my cousin DJ and told him about the whole situation with Braxton. He told me that if Braxton was looking at his third strike there was a possibility that he would do whatever it took to keep himself out of jail, even if it meant killing me so I wouldn't testify. Man, this situation had just gone from a 10-point situation to a 50!

DJ asked, "So what are you going to do?"

"Look, the only reason I called the police in the first place was because I thought the car was unable to start, and I didn't feel safe. I never meant for the situation to escalate to this. I don't wanna die over no bull ish."

He said, "I'll call the triple OG from Braxton's gang set and let him know that you will be dropping all charges, and Braxton will leave this situation alone and never contact you again."

About an hour later, I received a call from DJ saying that everything was all good, meaning Braxton and I had no beef. Unfortunately, I got a ten minute lecture from DJ. He explained that a square like me had no business being at a biker function, nor should I have been in South Central during that time of night. He told me, "You always have been book smart, but you ain't street smart, and there's a difference. You were out of your element by even being down in that part of town." He told me to no longer have contact with Braxton, and for my gullible ass not to go anywhere near the southeast side of LA. I felt like a kid getting scolded by my big cousin. Later on, I received another phone call from Braxton saying simply, "Thank you."

The next day, I called the police and dropped all charges. They seemed upset with me. However, I couldn't knowingly proceed with charges, since I played a hand in this entire mess too. My conscience wouldn't allow me to imprison a somewhat guilty man for that. The police did inform me that even though I was dropping the case, the DA still could pick it up. I explained to them I didn't care what happened at that point. I was just done with the situation, and would no longer be cooperating with them. I guess the case never made it to court, because from word on the street, Braxton is still a free man.

Although I did drop the case, I was still paranoid that Braxton would find me. I started doing the extreme. I was so paranoid that I wanted to make sure that I never ran back into him again, not even by accident. To ensure that he couldn't find me while riding through the streets of LA, I changed my personalized license plate to a standard DMV-issued plate, tinted my windows, and got some noticeable dinks in the car repaired. Any time someone would ask if I wanted to attend a motorcycle club function, my answer would be, "Hell no!" I didn't ever want to chance running into this man anytime soon, truce or not.

In all my years of pursuing the right to get even with a man for hurting me, lying to me, and/or cheating on me, I had never experienced something like this. It seemed surreal. I thought of all those times I had gone in the dark, even in broad daylight to slash tires, break windows, and vandalize cars. I had begun to think that I was untouchable, yet I was gullible when it came down to this situation. No man besides Mashon had ever retaliated by physically hurting me for hurting him or his property. This experience was definitely an eye opener on so many levels. As I sit here and write about this, I am just glad that I am able to still be alive to tell this story. I never thought that I would wind up experiencing something like this. It made me start to re-evaluate the caliber of men that I was meeting, how I was carrying myself. I questioned my judgment, and I was trying to figure it all out.

A situation like this…you never forget, and you learn to appreciate your life even more. I was spared that night while being taught a life lesson. It may sound crazy, but a year to the date of the assault and robbery, I looked in the mirror and ran my hand across the top of my right eyebrow to feel the scar from that fight. I reflected how much my life had changed behind that one night. If that hadn't happened, I think that I would still be down the road to self-destruction. It took something horrific to change my life. What a shame!

Sampson – Please Give Me Strength

After many years of having no communication with Garin, I ran into Vance, who was Garin's business partner back in the 90's. He recognized me right off the bat and said, "Hey, Kennedee, how are you doing?"

"I'm fine, how are you?" Of course my questions were all about how Garin was and where he was.

"I haven't seen Garin in a couple years. I've talked to him recently, but it's been a while since I've seen him," said Vance.

I reached into my purse and handed him my business card. "If you talk to Garin any time soon, please tell him to call me."

"I will," Vance agreed.

I walked away with a smile on my face because I was excited that I was going to finally be reunited with Garin after all these years. I was very disappointed when my phone never rang. After about two weeks, I realized that Garin probably wasn't going to call me. I put that on the back burner to pursue something else when it came along.

These social networking sites are something else. If someone sees you as someone else's friend, then they want to be your friend. All of a sudden, you have a million friends on your list that you don't even know. I don't play that. If I don't know you, then you are not getting on my page!

I made an exception for one person. I can recall getting a friend request from a man by the name of Sampson that I didn't know. He happened to be friends with a guy that I grew up with. I took a look at his page and was truly intrigued, as he had many pictures of him and celebrities. I went ahead against my better judgment and accepted the friend request. I emailed him to see what he was about, but all I got back was an email telling me to call him.

I did. The voice on the other line was deep and soothing. He sounded educated and mature. I asked, "How old are you?"

"I'm forty-five."

While sitting on the phone, I turned on the Internet, went to his page, and thought, *Well, he doesn't look forty-five.* So I proceeded with the conversation.

"Can you meet me for drinks in Westchester?" he asked.

I agreed.

When I arrived at this hidden cantina, I was not happy about meeting at a hole-in-the-wall establishment. I thought, *He could have chosen something better than this.* As I approached the entrance of the cantina, I saw Roland, my childhood friend that I had grown up with.

"What are you doing here?" Roland asked.

"I met someone off of your page, and he asked me out for drinks."

"Cool, well, he is waiting for you inside."

When I got into the restaurant, there he was sitting at the bar. He was dark chocolate with a bald head, and he was very handsome. As I made my way to the other side to sit down next to him, he stood up. It felt like a scratch record had just happened. This man was shorter than me. He stood about 5'5" and it might have been overly generous of me to say that, because I really want to say 5'4". I thought about turning around and just leaving, but he had already spotted me. I just played it off, smiled, and kept walking towards him.

"It's a pleasure to meet you," Sampson said sincerely. "You look just like all your pictures on my page."

I thought to myself, *You don't, though.* He was charming and undeniably had a swagger to him. He bought round after round after round. Next thing I know, I was too tipsy to drive all the way back home. He insisted I stay at his house. Now, don't get me wrong this is not something that I do on a regular, but I did take him up on his invitation. He arrived at his luxury apartment in Ladera Heights. He had the place furnished really nice, and it was clean too. That was a plus.

I slept in the bed and he slept on the couch. The next morning, we woke up and went to breakfast at Pann's. We had a pleasant conversation, considering it was so early in the morning. I was just wishing he would be quiet though, because I don't start fully functioning until after 10:00 a.m. I just sat there and pretended that I cared what he was saying.

"What are you doing later today?" Sampson asked.

"Nothing."

"Would you like to go out again?"

In the back of my mind, I heard myself yelling, "Hell no!" But when I opened my mouth, I heard the word "Yes" come out.

From that day forward, we spent every other day with each other. To keep it 100, I would say that I was only allowing him to entertain me because there was no one else in my life at the time. We went everywhere and did everything. It was like we were a couple. There is a difference in being a couple, and something *like* one. A couple doesn't talk to other people while the other one is sitting there, and if the person who is a part of a couple attempts to do it, they just might get shanked. Well, this man let me know on several occasions that we were not "together" like that.

I had met him over at Roland's house one night. They had just come back from eating at the Cheesecake Factory. They brought back doggie bags and some hoes. There was Sampson, Roland, two other guys, plus three unidentified women. As the women began to talk, I realized that they had just met at the Cheesecake Factory. Roland had a fabulous house, and was giving everyone a tour. I sat there mad as Sampson came down the stairs with one of these women on his back. He must have seen me give him the evil eye, because he quickly put her down.

Suddenly, some guy came up from behind me and asked me what my name was. I quickly put him in his place and let him know that I was there strictly for Sampson, which is the same thing that Sampson should have been doing instead of acting like a free-spirited hoe.

I had just recently started to indulge in alcohol; weed has never been my thing. Roland had the Patron shots pouring, though, and sticky-icky in the air. I'll have to blame everyone's actions on the alcohol or drugs, because everyone was touchy feely and overly-friendly with one another. I really got the feeling that if I wasn't there, an orgy would have popped off. Since I had known Roland for many years and he had ordained me his little sister, I think that he respected that, and kept it G-rated instead. Glad he did, because I don't play that.

As the night progressed, I heard one of the women ask, "Why is she here?" She meant me.

I looked over and said, "Did you have something you want to say to me?"

"I was just wondering who you were," she replied.

"I am actually here with Sampson and will be leaving here with him too."

Her jaw dropped. Her friends were looking at her in shock. See, that's one thing that I have learned throughout the years. You never let another woman think she got the upper hand on you. True enough, there may have been interest in her from him; however, after saying what I said to her, there was no way she was going to talk to him unless she was a trifling type of female. And she damn sure wasn't going to do it while I was standing there.

There are always signs to let you know when to stop dealing with a man. I just gave you an example. Nevertheless, sometimes you still continue to deal with them like I did. I continued to deal with Sampson, knowing that he had dog tendencies.

On one particular day, we were out at Magic Johnson's Friday's having a late dinner. I looked over to see him macking to another female. Now this time he was just blunt with it. The girl looked over, saw me, and told him she was cool. I'm thinking, *The NERVE of him!* On the other hand, I had no one but myself to blame because I somewhat allowed him to get away with it the first time at Roland's house. Then again, we still weren't in a relationship, so there was no loyalty or ownership.

From that day forward, our relationship with one another changed, if you even want to call it that. Christmas was approaching, since he was the only one that I was seeing, I asked, "Are we going to exchange gifts?"

"Yes."

"What do you want?"

He thought for a moment. "I want a Louis Vuitton carry-on."

I know you are probably sitting there like "What"? Cuz I know I was thinking that.

Sampson went on to explain, "I want a carry-on like the one that you have."

In return, I told him, "Well, I want a Gucci watch!"

These were some extravagant type of requests, yet this was nothing out of the ordinary because we were used to doing upscale things (minus Magic Johnson's Friday's). Now doing upscale dinners and lunches versus buying Louis & Gucci are two different things. There was no way in hell I was going to buy this fool no Louis Vuitton carry-on! He really had the game jacked up. I wasn't expecting the watch from him either, but I knew whatever he got me would be nice.

In early December, Sampson told me that he would be attending a fight in Las Vegas, but he didn't ask me to go. As that week approached, I thought maybe he would, but he still didn't. I decided to go to Vegas too. I contacted my best friend Taylor and asked her if she wanted to roll with me. She said yes. I let Sampson know the day before the fight that my girl and I would be up there too.

Sampson said, "Cool, just hit me once you guys get there, and I'll meet you somewhere."

On the Saturday of the fight, Taylor and I met at my Uncle Matthew's house and got on the 15 freeway. On the way to Vegas, I realized I had forgotten my jacket in my car.

Taylor said, "We can stop by an outlet mall on the way into Vegas."

When we arrived at the mall, I realized my phone had been in the trunk the whole time. I got the phone out and there were two missed calls and one text message from Sampson. The text read, "I'm not going to Vegas have a good time." I showed Taylor the text.

She said, "He lying!"

I frowned. "I know."

See, Sampson knew if he told me he wasn't coming to Vegas, he didn't have to hang out with me, which led me to believe that he was bringing someone (like another woman) with him, and he didn't want me to find out. I would usually hear from Sampson three or four times a day. After he sent that text, I tried calling several times throughout the day, and he wouldn't answer. But whenever I would send a text, he would reply maybe like ten minutes later. He knew he couldn't answer that phone because his trifling ass knew he was in Vegas too. It's hard to keep a lie going when you can hear the sound of slot machines and thousands of people in the background. So he kept it safe by texting me.

Taylor and I still went. We enjoyed our trip and went to the fight, hit up about three different clubs that night, and topped it off with a 6 a.m. Denny's breakfast before we hit the road right back to California. Even though I knew Sampson was in Sin City without me, I still made the best of the trip. I didn't trip out on him because remember, it's not what you know, but what you can prove. And even though I knew he was out there, I sure couldn't prove it.

A few weeks prior to Christmas, a co-worker gave me a $25 gift card to Bed, Bath & Beyond. I had no need for it, so I used it to buy Sampson some much-needed pots and pans. He only had one pot and one skillet, and that wasn't cutting it for me when it came to cooking. I bought him a dish rack drainer because he was using a towel on the countertop to let the dishes air dry. For this man to have a little money in his pocket, he sure wasn't choosing to spend it on things that were truly needed in his house.

I presented him with his new gifts. He seemed pleased until he opened his mouth and said, "You know I don't really cook."

I said, "I figured since I am over here so much that I would like to cook more often, and I need the proper tools."

He nodded. "Well thanks, I appreciate that."

I went by Sampson's place a few days later. I looked in the refrigerator to get a bottle of water only to find the new dishes that I had bought filled with someone else's cooking. There was macaroni & cheese, yams, and greens in the pans. There was also smothered chicken in the skillet. I was dumfounded. I wasn't sure what to say. I just took all the food and dumped it down the garbage disposal.

Sampson caught me in the middle of doing all that. "What do you think you're doing?"

I retorted, "What do you think *you're* doing? I didn't buy these damn pots and pans for you to invite some hussy over for her to cook for you. If she wanted to cook so bad for you, then her ass should have bought the pots and pans before I did."

He was speechless, and that worked for me. Some girl was there cookin' dinner in *my* pans? Ain't that a trip!

I was still uncertain about Sampson after the Las Vegas incident and after wasting a gift card on him. However, I still was talking to him. I still wanted to get him something nice for Christmas. I like to give unique gifts, things that people can remember me by. I enlisted the services of my cousin Aden, who was a painter. I gave her a picture of him and she made a painting.

On Christmas day, I was all excited to give him his gift. He opened it, and loved it. He handed me a box. I opened mine and hated it. This man had bought me some pajamas. They were bottoms that had "Merry Christmas" written all over it, and the top was a baby tank with "Merry Christmas" written across the front. I was heated, but all I could do was say, "Thanks so much!" In the back of my mind, I was thinking, *He probably bought this ish from Big Lots, and his cheap ass could have at least gone to Vickie's Secret.* There I stood with poor-quality cotton PJ's and he had a portrait ready to be hung over his fireplace. You tell me, who was winning in this scenario?

I sent a picture of me wearing my new PJ's to my girls, and we had laughs for days about them cheap-ass PJ's. I spent the night at his house that evening. When he left to go to work the next day, I rummaged through the cabinets and drawers, looking for something to eat. I ended up stumbling on several gift cards from several females that had given Sampson gifts for Christmas. I found PF Chang's, Benihana, Grand Lux Cafe, California

Pizza Kitchen, and many Starbucks cards. I took the PF Chang's and the Starbucks gift cards for myself. Ho! Ho! Ho! Merry Christmas to me! If he found them missing, I really doubted that he would have the gall to ask if I took them. After I spent that much money for his present and all I got were those cheap-ass PJ's, I really didn't feel bad about stealing the gift cards from him.

New Year's Eve was approaching and I asked Sampson his plans. He said, "I'm going to be in Vegas. Once again, I didn't get an invite, but I wasn't really tripping since I was brought up to either bring the New Year in at home or at church. I told him, "Bring me back a keychain."

"Okay," Sampson agreed.

On New Year's Eve, I was sitting home alone watching the *Law & Order* marathon when I got a text at 12:00 a.m. on the nose. It was from Sampson, and it read "Happy New Year." I looked at the phone and put it down. I just had this whatever attitude with him at that point.

The next day, I got on the Internet and found some random message from some chick off his friend's page, stating that I needed to leave him alone, and that she was with him last night. When I clicked on her page to see who this chick was, she had posted pictures from New Year's Eve with him. I guess you're wondering, how did I know they were from New Year's Eve? The bottom of the picture had a time and date stamp. The pictures sure didn't look like they were in Vegas. I was once again upset with this lil trifling man. I immediately called him, but there was no answer. I sent him one of those long texts explaining what had just happened. His reply was that he knew nothing about that, and he would call me later.

He did call me later and asked me to meet him for dinner to talk about things. When I arrived at the restaurant, he was already waiting. When I sat down, he said, "What, no hug or kiss?"

I said, "Oh, I think you have gotten enough of those over the past 24 hours."

"What is that supposed to mean?"

"You didn't have to lie!"

He looked perplexed. "What did I lie about?"

"You told me you were in Vegas for New Year's Eve when you were with some chick. Why would you lie?"

"I didn't lie; I had a change of plans."

I said, "Do not try to sit up here and play me for a fool! I swear I will turn this table over if you don't stop lying to me!"

He shrugged. "Turn the table over if you want to. I'll just leave."

"I don't care. It's not like I don't know where you live at."

Sampson narrowed his eyes. "Fine, you want the truth?"

"That's why I am here."

"I went up north to the bay area to go visit a friend. I had already made plans with her prior to meeting you. It's not like we are together."

"Well, why lie to me like we are together?" He just sat there with this stupid look on his face. At that very moment, that should have been my exit, but I continued to stay on this roller coaster ride.

We continued to see one another, yet I was trying to figure out how to leave him all along. Valentine's Day was approaching, and this would be the first time in a long time that I wouldn't be spending it alone. We went to this lovely restaurant in Culver City. He ended up paying over $300 for our meal for that evening. He redeemed himself from that whole Christmas disaster. We were back on good terms and things seemed to be okay.

The next month would be his birthday. Since he did attempt to fix his gift-giving failure from Christmas, I decided to reward him with a nice gift for his birthday. I asked what he wanted. I should have learned from the previous time not to ask, yet I still did. This time he said he wanted to go to some designer store at the Beverly Center.

On his birthday, we went to the store. Now when he said Beverly Center, I should have known that this was going to be an expensive gift. He acted as if he was in a candy store. He was picking up shirts that cost $200, $150, $ 100…

I had to say, "Hey, slow your roll, I am not spending no more than $100 on you!"

Sampson proceeded to the sales rack. He found two shirts that came to a total of $90. I just couldn't allow him to break my pockets too much since we didn't have a real commitment to each other.

I asked if he was going to be doing something else for his birthday, maybe for the weekend or something. Sampson said, "No, I'm not really into celebrating birthdays."

I thought, *So why the hell did I just spend $90 on two shirts that weren't for me?*

Sampson continued to speak. "As you get older, birthdays are just another day."

The next day I went to his page to see what birthday wishes his other female friends were wishing him. One particular girl left a comment, so I clicked on her page, and he had left a comment back thanking her for the birthday wishes and inviting her to his birthday party at this lounge in Beverly Hills on Saturday. I was like err... what the hell??? I thought he said he wasn't doing anything? I tell you, a man will try to outwit, outplay, and outsmart me, but in the end, I will have the last laugh.

My first thought was to call him out on the carpet for lying to me, but that would be too easy. Instead, I immediately started getting my crew together to go with me to crash this party. After I assembled the crew, I made hair and nail appointments for Saturday. I got my hair done and my fingernails and feet. My intent was to definitely have the men on pause when I walked into the room. After I finished with my appointments, I went to the mall to get a cute outfit. I bought a pink and black halter top, which was very pretty, some mini black shorts, and strappy black heels. I must say, I was looking good.

The crew consisted of my girls: Taylor, Neena, my cousin Kayla, and my homeboy Jacari. My cousin Kayla invited some of her crew too, which consisted of four other young ladies and four gentlemen. We came in deep.

I was getting too much attention when we came into the door. Those shorts with my long legs made for a deadly combination, especially since we were still in the winter season. Guys were approaching us left and right at the bar, and I hadn't even made my rounds around the lounge to see if he was there. Turns out I didn't have to look for him, because all the commotion over the girls and me from getting hit on at the bar caused him to look and see what was going on. Before he could fully approach the bar, our eyes connected. He couldn't do anything but lower that sorry head of his. He knew he was caught.

The crew and I sat down in the center of the lounge while he was near back in the corner. He had a good view of us. I saw him every now and again looking over at us, but he never made his way over to speak because he had a date with him. It was the same girl off his page who had contacted me, letting me know about her. Mocha Diva was this chick from the Bay Area that was about forty years old. She didn't come dressed like she was with the birthday boy. She dressed more like she was coming from church. She had on some black wrap dress, some Payless shoes from 2003, and a synthetic half-wig on. She stood about two inches taller than me, which made him look like a midget standing next to her. She had no swagger to her whatsoever, yet he chose for her to be on his arm for his party.

Sampson must have known the club owner, because all of a sudden, I heard the music stop and some guy saying that they wanted to give a shout out to Sampson for his birthday. He invited Sampson up on the stage. Why was this man wearing the shirt that I just bought him to his birthday party? It took all I had within me to keep from ripping that shirt right off his back. The guy went on to say that there was a special lady in the house that he heard could sing like a hummingbird, and that he wanted her to come and sing Happy Birthday to Sampson.

Oh my goodness, up walks Mocha Diva, getting the microphone handed to her! By that time, I had had about four shots of Patron yet I wouldn't blame my upcoming behavior on the alcohol. As soon as she belted out the first note of Happy Birthday, I began to boo her. I then tried to get my folks to do the same. A few joined in while others seemed a bit embarrassed.

At that point, I really didn't care. I felt as if Mocha Diva and Sampson should have been glad that's all my drunken butt was doing was booing. After my booing session, I went into the ladies room with Neena and Taylor. We were fixing our hair and makeup when Mocha Diva walked in. I looked at her, and she looked at me. She walked by and went into the bathroom stall.

Right before she closed the bathroom stall, she yelled, "Stupid bitch!"

Keep in mind that we were the only ones in the restroom, so I knew she was talking about me. I told her, "You a coward, bitch! How you going to call me a bitch behind a closed door? You're a scary bitch. You talked all that shit on the Internet. Why don't you come out that stall and we will see who the bitch is?"

By this time, Neena was fired up and you could hear her saying, "Yeah, bitch, come out the stall!"

On the other hand, Taylor has always been the punk in the crew, and she was trying to simmer the situation down by dragging me out of the ladies room. Thinking back on that night, I'm glad Taylor did drag me out of there. Otherwise, Neena, Mocha Diva, and I probably would have been in jail that night.

Fifteen minutes later, my folks and I were out the door. I was so drunk that I had to call Jackson to come get me from where we all met and parked our cars. He wasn't too happy about having to come get me at two o'clock in the morning, but he came anyway. The next morning, he dropped me off at Kali's house. I spent the morning with her chatting it up with her about how this old man had cut up at the club. Later on, Taylor picked me up from Kali's house and took me back to my car.

When I got to my car, I couldn't find the keys. I rummaged all through my purse, but no keys. I went back to Kali's house in search for the keys and didn't turn up with anything. I called Jackson. "Please look around your place and your car and see if you can find my keys!"

He called back. "I didn't find anything, but I will let you know."

I was so upset. This whole scenario had turned into a catastrophe of a weekend. I told Taylor, "Drop me off at the Marriott." I got a room and settled in for the night, because come Monday morning, I was going to have to go the dealership to have a new key made. By nine o'clock that night, Jackson had called to tell me that he found my keys. He told me that his landlady found them lying by the gate. He came to the hotel and dropped them off. By that time, I had already been in the room for about five hours, so I just stayed the night.

The next day, I called into work and let them know that I was going to be late. I checked out of the hotel and went over to Sampson's job. I was so angry that this little man had played me, but I had no one to blame but myself. I couldn't allow him to think that his current or previous behavior was acceptable. I allowed myself one whole day to cool off before I talked to him. I know one day doesn't really sound reasonable, but this was a big step for me, because previously, we just would have had that conversation that night right there in the middle of the club with all hell breaking loose.

I showed up to discuss with him what happened on Saturday night. I asked, "Why did you lie to me again?"

"Lie about what?"

I frowned. "About the party!"

Sampson shook his head. "I didn't."

"Yes you did!"

He waved his hand dismissively. "The party wasn't something special."

"Why didn't you invite me?"

"I wanted to have someone there that wasn't going to trip on me having my other female friends there."

What he really meant was, "I had all the chicks I am having sex with there, and don't need anybody there that was going to trip." All he did was add fuel to the fire. I told him, "You had the nerve to have the shirt on that I just bought you, yet I wasn't invited to the party? I felt like ripping that shirt right off your back!"

"I don't like the way the conversation is going, and I don't appreciate the indirect threats."

"Well, luckily for you, I have learned how to use my words, because before, my hands would have been all over you — and I don't mean that in a good way."

"What does that mean?" he asked angrily.

I replied, "It means the old me would have just socked you in the lip by now! However, I am standing here voicing my concerns to you instead. I'm not going to put up with this bull-ish anymore!" I turned away and proceeded to the car. I never called, emailed, or texted him again.

He did send a text message to me a month later talking about "Happy Resurrection Day". All I did was look at my phone, put it back down, and commence to eating. That was the last I heard of him.

I felt very proud of myself for not tearing up his ride or assaulting him. Don't think that it didn't come across my mind, but the difference was that I never acted on those thoughts. No matter what I did to him, it could not replace the months that I spent trying to make something out of nothing with this man, or the money I spent on gifts for the little dwarf. It actually made me feel better to be able to walk away without reprimanding him for his actions. I couldn't allow him to continue to think he was more important than what he was by acting a complete fool just to get even. At that very moment, I realized that I had grown up and become a real woman.

Jackson – The Last Round

By this time, I had realized that Jackson had turned into my safety cushion and go-to guy. Whenever I didn't have anyone in my life, I knew that Jackson could fill that void. This time around, Jackson had left Shay and was living in an apartment by himself. It wasn't in the best neighborhood, but I was glad that he finally had stepped up and was becoming a man.

Even though Jackson had a good job, he never had any money. He was always broke, and I was always having to pay for stuff. He could get away with that because even in our 30's, he was still fine.

One day, he left me at the house by myself. For many that know me, they would have told him that that wasn't a good idea. What woman doesn't go through a man's stuff when given a chance? It gives one the opportunity to find out more information about someone that may be good or bad.

That's exactly what I did when he left me there by myself. I started rummaging through his drawers. I came upon a letter that Shay had written him. In the letter, she stated that she didn't want him in her house any longer. She was giving him 60 days to get out. By law, she was only required to give him 30 days, but she said she was being generous with the 60 days. She said she had had enough of him coming in the house at all hours of the night, or not coming home at all, and just acting like it was all good between them. She went on to say how hurt she was that he had another child outside of their relationship. Apparently, Shay intended on naming their first child Lexi, and he had named the other little girl the name that they had picked out. Shay said she couldn't take it anymore. After all that he had put her through, she was fed up with him and it was time for him to go, that he could no longer use her.

I was floored after reading that letter. I couldn't believe it! Well, I guess I could, because after all the things that he put me through, I could see him doing the same to Shay. I was just so upset with him that he had not even told me that he had fathered a third child. I guess he knew that if he told me, I would have been very upset since he made it seem like I couldn't have a child by him, because it would put him into a deeper financial hole. So this was the reason why he was out on his own. He had got caught cheating and lying in the worst way.

I put everything back like I found it, locked the front door, and left. I got a phone call later from him. He asked, "Why did you leave before I got back?"

"I was tired and I needed to get back home." He said he understood.

I waited for a few weeks to pass, thinking that maybe he would say something about him having the little girl, but he didn't say anything. On Monday, I finally texted him. The text read: "When were you going to tell me about your daughter?"

He texted back, "When you needed to know."

I fired back, "When was that?"

He responded with "I'm not sure."

I texted, "How old is she?"

"Two years old," he responded, which meant he was messing with me and somebody else at the same time, but it wasn't a surprise. I continued to deal with Jackson even though I knew of his circumstances. We had been in an eleven-year-long on-and-off again relationship and it was harder to just walk away, even though I know I should have. I feel like I had invested so much time in Jackson. He was growing up and he was turning out to be a better friend than he had been in the beginning stages of our relationship, which made it hard for me to stop loving him.

There was only one other person who made me feel this way, and it was Garin. He never had reached out to contact me, and it seemed as if I was the only one that was looking for him. I didn't want to give up on Garin, even though I had no way of finding him. So I turned to the best way of finding someone: the Internet. I used Google to search for Garin. A lot of searches came up with his discography. That's not what I was looking for, because I already knew what hits he had already made. I needed more detailed information, like where he lived, his telephone number, his cell phone number, something concrete to get me in contact with him. I even did a people search by paying money, but the addresses and phone numbers that it retrieved were no good.

I thought, *There has to be something on this Internet about him.* I looked up a website of a company that Garin now owned. They didn't have an address or telephone number on how to reach him, but it did have links to MySpace. I clicked on the MySpace link, which led me to his profile – or so I thought. Instead, it was the company's profile. There was still no information on how to contact them. I looked at his top friends to see if I saw anyone that I recognized. Unfortunately, I didn't recognize any of the names or faces.

I clicked on his first friend, and he had his company information listed. I called the number, and it was a white guy who answered. I said, "Hi, I am trying to get in contact with Garin Baptise."

He said, "Sure, let me get his number."

I was shocked at how easy this one phone call turned out to be. He got back on the phone and gave me the number. I said, "Thank you so much, and have a good night!" That went more smoothly than I thought! I was certain that this guy would have asked who I was or what I wanted with Garin. I was excited yet anxious to finally have some type of way to contact him.

The first night that I had his information, I did not even utilize it. I had to contemplate how I was going to approach him, since that it had almost been eight years since we last talked. I had to get my mindset together just in case he was with someone else or didn't even want to deal with me again. The next day, I picked up the phone, blocked my cell phone number, and I called him. He didn't answer, so I hung up.

I called later on that evening, again with the number blocked. He still didn't pick up. So this time I left a message trying to disguise my voice. I said, "Hey, just wanted to call and see how you are doing. Give me a call back when you can." I did that on purpose so he would be like, "Who is this, and how do I reach them?" I was kind of hoping that he would recognize my voice, because I have such distinctiveness to my voice that people always seem to know it's me when I call.

I waited a couple hours, then I called him back with my number revealed. This time he answered the phone. I said, "Hey, how are you?"

"Who is this?"

"It's Kennedee."

"Who?"

"Kennedee."

He paused. "Let me call you right back."

My heart felt like it dropped down to the bottom of my stomach. When he said that, I was so disappointed. I just knew that he wasn't happy to hear from me and that he wasn't going to call me back.

About an hour passed by. The phone rang, and there was no number on the caller ID. I answered the phone and he said, "Hey, girl. How have you been?"

It was a different tone than what he previously had when he answered earlier, and it made me more confident that he was happy to hear from me. I explained that I had decided back in 2000 to go back to school for my degrees. "I now have my associate's degree in child development. I have my bachelor's degree in business, and I'm working on my master's degree in social work. I'm now working for a non-profit organization as an executive associate, which means nothing, but I am a supervisor to some crappy people. Are you still producing?"

He said, "Here and there."

"Where do you live?"

"I live in LA right now."

"Oh, okay. Well, I'm back in the Inland Empire area still."

Garin said, "You're still out there?"

"Yes, I'm here, just trying to make it happen for myself."

"Do you come to LA often?" he asked.

"I'm out there all the time," I told him.

Garin paused. "How did you find me?"

I explained the story to him, and he seemed somewhat mortified at the fact that someone would just give out his information without asking questions. I agreed that it was crazy how that guy just gave out his information, but it did benefit me, so I could care less.

Garin asked, "Do you have any recent pictures of yourself?"

I laughed. "Why, are you trying to see if I got fat or not? I still look the same."

"How do I know that?"

"You have to trust me."

"Let me see some pictures," he cajoled me. He gave me his e-mail address and I e-mailed some pictures to him. He said, "Oh my God, you have gotten so grown and gorgeous!"

"You're making me blush!" To hear the word "gorgeous" come from his mouth was truly a compliment because I knew that he had dealt with so many beautiful women working in the music industry. I asked, "Do you have any pictures of yourself that you can e-mail me?"

He told me, "Go to the MySpace site, go to the search box, put in my e-mail address, and you can find me."

So I did that, and to my surprise, I was glad to see the same guy and that I had met when I was eighteen years old. He was still as handsome as ever. He asked me, "Would you like to meet?"

I didn't want to sound too excited. "Sure. What day did you have in mind?"

"How about Friday evening?" he suggested.

I said, "Sounds good to me!" He gave me an address to meet him at along with a time. I had two days to get myself ready to go meet him and make my first impression for the second time.

That Friday I called out sick from work. I went and got my hair done, my nails done, and I got a pedicure. I was ready to go see him. I was so nervous on my drive down to LA. I wanted to make sure that I looked good, smelled good, and said all the right things. It was like being eighteen all over again, but this time, I wouldn't be intimidated by his maturity.

I arrived at the address that he gave me. It turned out to be a studio. I called to let him know that I was outside. He said he would be right out. While I was waiting in the car, I began to fix my hair and makeup, making sure the finished product was perfect before he came out. I knew I only had one chance, and I wasn't going to blow it this time.

Garin came walking out the doors, and my heart started to pound. He looked exactly the same. He wasn't fat. He was well put together still. I got out of the car, walked over to him, and he immediately hugged me. We squeezed each other tight for a good two minutes.

Garin said, "It's really good to see you!"

"It's good to be seen, and it's good to see you as well!"

We walked into the studio. We sat down on the couch, and he said, "You know, I just can't get over how gorgeous you have turned out to be!"

I laughed. "Dang, was I that ugly when I was younger?"

He smiled. "No, you weren't ugly at all, you were just young."

"Well thanks, darling, I appreciate the compliment." That meant a lot coming from him.

"My pleasure!"

We sat there and we talked for hours. I had originally intended to only stay there for about forty-five minutes because I was supposed to be meeting Jackson for dinner. However, I ended up staying there with him for probably about 2 ½ hours, just talking, reminiscing, laughing, and getting to know each other all over again. We could both tell that we were happy to see one another.

As much as I wanted to stay cool and calm, I could tell I was nervous. Anytime I get nervous, my palms start sweating. But I kept my composure, and he never knew that I was nervous around him. I finally told him, "I have to go. I have plans and I have people waiting for me."

Garin seemed as if he didn't want me to leave. That was definitely a good sign. I told him I had to go, and I would call him later. He said okay, and walked me to the car, and gave me a kiss on the cheek.

I later arrived at Jackson's house, and he seemed mad that I was a little late, but he required no explanation. I just told him I had gotten stuck in traffic. Throughout the night, I got several texts from Garin. He wanted to know what I was doing later on that night and if I could see him. I told him no, that I was busy, but maybe later on that weekend. From the texts that I received from Garin, I could tell that I had his attention. Finally! It took me time to become a woman to get his attention, but I had it. And this time I would make sure that I'd keep it.

Unfortunately, it would be a whole month before we would see each other again. We made plans to go on a date to the Santa Monica pier. We just walked around talking and holding hands. I had questions for him, like what type of women he was used to dating, what he was looking for in a relationship... I just needed to know because I did not want to go into this blind.

Garin told me that he liked professional women, classy women who had their own things going on. That sounded like me so far. Then he hit me with the hardest words to swallow. "I'm not really looking for a relationship."

That was a little hurtful to me, because I knew that I wanted to be in a relationship. That's what I was looking for. I knew that's what I wanted, and it's hard to deal with someone that's not on that page. I kept quiet. I tend to do that when I'm upset. It's better for me to just not say anything than to sit there and try to say something nice and maybe have it turn out to be mean or hurtful.

Garin said, "What's wrong?"

"Nothing." I tried to shrug it off.

"Are you sure?"

"I'm sure."

"You got quiet after I said that," he probed.

"I will be honest, I do want to be in a relationship, but I mean, I can't say that it's going to happen right now with you. But it is something that I would like to pursue later on."

"Well, that's something we could discuss. I'm not closed to the idea, but I'm just not looking for anything."

He smoothed things over with that statement, and I was able to continue to enjoy the night. We went to El Torito's in Santa Monica for dinner. Turned out he didn't drink, but that was okay, because I did. I had a couple of margaritas, we both had entrées, and by the end of the night, I was feeling a little frisky. I was rubbing on his leg underneath the table to let him know that I was interested in doing something else besides holding hands.

When we walked out to the car, he turned around, grabbed me, and started kissing me passionately on my neck. Then he slobbed me down with a kiss on the mouth. He turned me on with that one. I murmured, "Let's go somewhere."

We were close to his studio, so we went there. We fell asleep in each other's arms. It felt so good to be in his arms after all this time. The next morning we woke up, and I dropped him off at home. He kissed me goodbye and told me he would call me later, and he did. I knew that if he was seeing someone else that I was not going to be able to deal with that; I needed to have him all to myself. I had desired him all those years, and I was damned if I was going to share him with someone else. When he called, I let him know just like that.

Garin said, "I told you that I wasn't ready for a relationship right now. I have a lot going on."

I guess I thought after making love to him it would somehow seal the deal with a relationship. But at that point I decided that I would just keep Garin and Jackson at the same time, because between the two of them, they were both doing their own thing. Why shouldn't I have the freedom to do so also?

So that is what I did. I kept them both in rotation, and neither one knew about the other. Garin and I would have sex and go out and I would make sure that he used a condom. Jackson and I were doing the same thing, but unfortunately, without a condom. By the time July had come, I didn't have a period. I wasn't quite sure what to think of it since I was spotting a little. I was hoping that I wasn't pregnant again by Jackson, as that was just ridiculous and redundant.

At the end of the month, I ended up going on vacation for my birthday, but by that time I figured I definitely was pregnant. Throughout my trip to Miami and the Bahamas I felt like crap. I was tired, I was not in a good mood, and I was also spotting, which wasn't a good sign.

When I got home from vacation the first thing I did was go to the doctor and get a pregnancy test. Turns out I was two months pregnant, and I knew who the daddy was. I called Jackson to let him know that I was pregnant again. I explained that I needed for him to take some time off from work so that we could go down to the clinic.

He got very, very angry with me, but how can he be angry when he knew he was not using a condom and I wasn't on the Pill? He was on the phone acting like he and I had never gone through this routine before. Why he was acting stupid all over again was a surprise to me. I thought he had grown up, and would be able to handle this a lil more maturely. I was so disgusted with him. He was getting on my nerves acting like it was my fault when he played a role in the situation too.

I told him, "Look, all you have to do is take me, and that's it. It's not like I'm asking you to shell out a dime of your money. I got this!"

Two weeks later, I made an appointment to terminate the pregnancy. My Aunt Tonya met me at Jackson's house, where I dropped my car off while he was at work. She then dropped me off at the clinic and I signed in. They took me in to do my paperwork. I found out that my insurance company had not even faxed over the claim form to approve me to get the surgery done. I was so upset I had to pay money out of pocket. I really didn't want to pay for it out of pocket when the insurance company was supposed to cover it, but I had already taken the day off from work. I figured I better just get it done while I was there. I put it on my credit card, and they took me in.

It was the same protocol. Nothing had changed over the years: weigh in, change clothes, put on some funny-looking blue shoes. They take your blood, and afterwards you're treated to Tylenol and nasty juice and crackers. They send you home with antibiotics and tell you they'll see you in two weeks. They call the person that is waiting for you in the waiting room and have them wait for you in the hallway.

There was Jackson waiting for me with his signature question. "How are you feeling?"

"I had to shell out the $400 because my insurance company did not fax over my paperwork."

"Why didn't you just wait?"

"I cannot call off another day! I just came back from vacation and I had to get this done today." I was getting bigger and I was only two and half months pregnant. I already gained fifteen pounds, and it was all in my stomach. People were beginning to ask questions. I had to get the procedure done so that my family and people at work could stop speculating about the possibility of me being pregnant.

I was just so irritated with Jackson because he did not once ask if he could do anything to help me. That was the least he could do! He never had to shell out a dime, and the one time money had to be shelled out, he never even offered to help compensate. I said, "You can't even ask if I need anything?" As we were driving on the freeway I just got so upset with him for not stepping up to the plate and being a better person at that moment. I let him know. "You know, never once have I asked you for a thing. You could at least say, 'Kennedee, let me give you something on it'."

Jackson yelled back at me, "I don't have anything to give to you! I don't have any money! If I had something, I would give it to you!" He then smacked the shit out of me.

Here I was just getting off of the abortion table for his raggedy ass, and all he can do is be upset with me and put his little slimy hands on me. I was so appalled that after eleven years of friendship and being in an on and off relationship that he had the nerve to put his hands on me of all days. Out of all the things that I have been through with him and all the things that I had done to him, he finally had the balls to try to stand up for himself.

Unfortunately, he chose the wrong situation for that. I was highly upset. I must've turned around and smacked him right back. I told him, "Pull this car over!"

He said, "No, I'm taking you to my house."

"I bet you will be sorry that you did!" I began to cry.

"I didn't even hit you that hard!" he scoffed.

"That was not cool!" I yelled. It wasn't until we got back to his house that he finally apologized for hitting me. It was too little too late. He would never place his hands on me again, and that I could guarantee.

When we arrived at his house, I went into the bathroom. I was surprised that I was bleeding so much and I was cramping really badly. I decided to still stay against my better judgment. I hopped in the shower to relax myself. When I got out, he had gone to McDonald's and gotten me my favorite Big Mac meal with an orange soda. I ate and took the antibiotics that the clinic had given me, and also took some pain pills that would help put me to sleep.

I woke up probably about four hours later. I asked him to go to the store to go get me a soda and some chips. He went and came back very quickly. Around 12 o'clock, he began to get dressed for work. I looked at him and said, "I thought that both of us were taking off work?"

Jackson shook his head, "I can't afford to take off."

"So you are going to leave me here by myself?"

"I cannot afford to take off work like you," he repeated.

All he did was add fuel to the burning fire. I was just so upset that he was going to leave me there by myself. I didn't care if it was only for a couple hours. It was the fact that he didn't have to do anything except be there, and he chose to use work as an excuse.

Jackson got dressed and he went to work. The next morning when I woke up, I rummaged through his stuff again. It had been a couple months since the last time I went through his things. This time I found a paycheck stub in his sock drawer. He was getting child support taken out for more than just two children. He had previously told me that his first son's mother hadn't filed child support on him. It was only his second son's mother and I was guessing the little girl's mom that had it out on him, so I didn't think too much of it. I just thought that maybe the first mom had taken out child support on him finally.

I saw that he was only bringing home about $300-$400 a week. However, he was making $1000 a week. I could see why he never had any money, and no wonder he couldn't afford to take off of work! It's hard to take care of yourself, pay bills, car note, insurance and pay rent and survive on $1,200 a month. It seems like he was just working to pay child support. He was actually making some decent money, but he wasn't seeing a dime of it. I felt sorry for him. However, he had brought all of this upon himself. A $4.00 pack of condoms could have solved all his problems, yet he wanted to be a nasty dog and just sleep with everyone without any protection.

As I was going through his things, I found a spare set of keys to his car. I kept the key for my own insurance purposes. When he got home, I acted as if everything was all right. I said, "I'm getting ready to go. I'll talk to you soon."

He walked me to the car. I got in and I went to breakfast with a friend at the Cheesecake Factory. Two weeks later, it was time for my check-up. I called Jackson to let him know that he needed to go with me. I know he didn't have to go with me at all, but I wanted him to be responsible in some kind of way and take some responsibility for his actions and help out. But he told me he couldn't go and if he could, he would let me know. The day before, I called to see if Jackson had changed his mind about going. He claimed he couldn't go because he had to work overtime. I went to my appointment, and everything was fine.

Afterwards, I went over to Magic Johnson's Friday's for Happy Hour to kill some time. I had sat down at the bar area. Someone came up from behind and said, "Can I buy you a drink, sexy?"

I turned around to see who it was. Sampson! Ugh! I was not happy at all to see him. This was my first time seeing or speaking to him since his birthday fiasco. He sat down next to me and said, "You still drink silver Patron?"

"I sure do!"

He called the bartender over and ordered shots of Silver Patron chilled.

While we waited for the drink order, he made small talk. He asked how I had been, what I had been up too, and what I was doing out in LA. I kept my answers short and sweet. I didn't give a damn that he was buying me a drink. It didn't change the fact that he was a liar.

Sampson said, "There is something that I would like to say to you."

"What is that?"

He whispered, "I'm sorry."

"What? I can't hear you?"

He cleared his throat. I said I am sorry."

"Sorry for what?"

"For everything. You are a good woman, and you deserved to be treated with respect. I didn't do that when I was with you, and for that I am sorry."

My heart should have softened at that moment, but it was too little too late. I didn't want to hear that bullshit now. He owed me that apology about five months ago. I said, "Well, Sampson, I guess." That's all I could say. I just didn't have the same feelings for him anymore and could care less if we ever mended our friendship.

Sampson was generous for the next few hours, buying me shots. I finally told him that I had to go. He said, "Why don't we go over to Paco Taco's?"

"No, I have some business that I need to handle."

"Well, it was really good to see you. You know where to find me."

I felt like telling him...yeah, in hell! Instead, I just smiled and said, "Have a good night."

You gotta know your worth as a woman before you're gonna be of any value to a man. Both Sampson and I had realized my worth, but unfortunately for him, it was too late. I really did have some business to take care of, since that whole day, Jackson never once called me.

I texted Jackson when I got in the car. "Where are you?"

He texted back, "I hurt my finger at work, and I am at Urgent Care."

I drove past his house, but his car wasn't there. I texted him back and said "Are you okay? Did you drive yourself or did someone take you?"

He replied, "I had to drive myself here."

I just somehow knew that he was lying. I turned the corner by his house and started driving down the street. Guess what I found? Jackson's Tahoe sitting on the next street. I texted back and said "What time do you think you will be done?"

He answered, "I don't know."

What a little liar! My intentions were to leave Jackson's keys back where I found them if I was able to get back into the house. However, once he tried to play me to the left AGAIN, my game plan changed.

I got out of the car and made my way to his apartment. I walked up the stairs, and you could hear music playing. I knocked on the door, but there was no answer. I waited; still no answer. I knocked on the door again, but this time with the police knock (you know, the kind that has the authority sound that makes you wanna say "who is it?") Still no answer. I turned around and used my foot to bang on the door. Still no answer, yet the music somehow turned itself down.

I yelled, "I know you're in there! You wanna play, let's play, but I bet you won't be laughing later!"

I started walking down the stairs. When I got to the gate, I turned to look at his apartment, and the blinds were moving. I knew his ass was in there. I got in my car, drove it ten blocks away, and parked it there. I looked in my trunk, got some gloves, and put them into my pocket. I started walking back toward Jackson's truck. I opened the door, got in, and started the car. I drove his car about another five blocks away from his house. I started going through all his stuff in the car before I abandoned it. I found pictures of girls, all kinds of girls: black girls, white girls, Asian girls, Mexican girls, all kinds of pictures. Some were pretty girls, and some were ugly girls. I guess he didn't have a preference at all as long as they had a v jay-jay.

Jackson had all kinds of papers in his car. A few were letters from girls expressing their undying love for him. Other papers were regular mail and legal papers. I opened up one of the letters from Department of Child Support Services. It was a letter letting him know that he had to pay X amount of dollars for his son. However, the child's name listed on the letter wasn't any of the kids that I knew about. This child was actually five years old, which meant that he actually had four children and not just three. I was flabbergasted and hurt. This low-down dirty, lustful man had been just sticking his little peter in anything that moved. I was literally disgusted. I got sick to my stomach and started throwing up. I had opened up the car door just in time for it not to get inside of his truck.

I regained my composure and I thought, I can't leave the truck here now. *What if they gather my vomit for my DNA?* Yeah, like a CSI crew would come out to gather DNA for a stolen truck. What was I thinking? I was paranoid. I was always thinking out of the ordinary when it came to doing my dirty work. I think that's why I ended up staying out of the arms of the law after that whole Ryan ordeal.

I started up the truck and parked it another five blocks away. I had to walk all the way back to my car. On that walk back, I thought of when I first unlocked the door to take the truck, and how remorseful I felt. I thought about the promise that I made to myself that I would no longer take matters into my own hands to get even. Then when I found those child support papers on that other kid, it took all the guilt away. Jackson better be lucky that's all I did was move it a few blocks away from his house, still within finding distance, because another part of me really wanted to torch that mug just like Angela Bassett did in *Waiting to Exhale*. On the way home, I tossed the keys on the freeway to keep myself from being tempted to go do anything else to his truck. I knew I would get a call or text from him when he realized his truck was missing.

Around ten o'clock that night, I received a text from Jackson. He said "I'm going to get you back."

I texted, "You wanna get back with me, I thought we were already together?"

He replied, "Don't act stupid, you know what I am talking about. If I have to spend the rest of my life, I am getting you back. I will."

I texted back, "Then bring it because you know I ain't never scared."

Later on in the middle of the night, the phone rang. I answered, and it was Jackson, sounding pitiful. He said, "Can I at least get my keys back?" I started laughing and hung up the phone.

Jackson had no idea where I lived at. I would always go to his house because mine was too far. Plus, I never stayed in one place for too long, because eventually, something or someone will end up catching up to you. The Internet makes it so easy for anyone to find anyone nowadays.

The next day, I changed my cell phone number, not because I was scared, but because we had done this same dance for too long. All those years of breaking up and and getting back together only to find that all of was worthless... He claimed that he loved me, and hell, according to some of those letters, he loved some other women too, but ultimately, he loved himself more than anything else. He had gotten away with far too much for far too long. For me, the scorecard was now even. I was ready to finally call it quits with Jackson after eleven years. It was time to move on.

I haven't spoken to Jackson since I moved his truck, although I have seen him. My godparents live about two blocks away from his parent's house. I have passed by the street where his parents live on numerous occasions at various times. Looks as if Jackson is back living at home with his parents at the age of thirty-five. I guess his playa days have caught up with him financially, and it is a hardship to remain an independent adult.

In some ways, I feel sorry for him, and in others, I don't. Some of the things that he is going through are because he brought them on himself. A lot of his problems could have been solved with a $4.00 pack of condoms. Instead, he got kids all over the place by all these different women. He shook up my mentality about me being so trusting even if I am in a monogamous relationship. Instead of getting tested for AIDS/HIV yearly, I get tested every six months. He exposed me to so much more than just getting my heart broken, and for that, I can never, ever forgive him.

My Time Has Come

W hen I rekindled with Garin, I was still dating Jackson. However, once that incident with Jackson took place, I decided to give my full attention to Garin. After Garin and I had our first sexual encounter in more than eight years, we didn't have sex again until six months later. Once again, it solidified that our relationship wasn't just about sex. I was even honest with him when I got pregnant the last time by Jackson. Even though he wanted to choke me out, we still were able to work things out. I ended up moving to LA the final time to be closer to Garin.

Never in my wildest dreams would I ever think that Garin and I would be a couple. He had come into my life at the worst time, but ended up being there for me all the time. He had seen me go through a lot and was there to pick up the pieces. After I stopped chasing the wrong things, I gave the right things a chance to catch up to me.

My life has now begun to settle down. It's been four years since Garin and I reunited. We have had our ups and downs. It hasn't been an easy road. I love Garin with all my heart. He disappoints me at times, but he isn't prideful and always apologizes when he has wronged me. I still have certain insecurities because of all the baggage that I have tried not to bring into the relationship. There are times when his phone rings in the middle of the night and he will put it on speaker to calm my fears, or if a text is received in the middle of the night, he will show me the text. These are things that I can appreciate because it helps me remain secure in our relationship.

Though Garin is no longer making the money that he used to, I still love him the same. I was never there because of his fame, which was the one thing that kept me from trying to pursue him. I think that if we had gotten back together back in the day, he would have been a part of my "romances that failed" chapters. I appreciate the man that he has become. He definitely has no full idea of some of my past adventures, although he is dying to read this book. I think it's best that the past should remain as it is: the past.

My life has changed drastically over the last four years. The things that I did previously are no longer acceptable to me. It's funny how people want to keep me in the same box despite the changes that I have made in my life. I still have friends that call me "crazy" or "psycho" because they experienced most of these stories with me, either by me telling them or them riding along with me for the ride. Some conspired with me to get revenge on some of these men, and seek assistance from me to plot against their men. For those who still like to blurt out that I'm crazy or psycho, I have to remind them of the good old days, and the roles they played at helping me make bad decisions while we were together. I know that I am no longer that person. You won't catch me climbing fences, doing drive by's, stakeouts, or destroying anyone's personal property.

First off, I am too old to be doing any of that, and I don't have the patience any longer. Secondly, what is done in the dark will eventually come to light. I listen to my intuition; it's cheaper than bail. Lastly, I am too classy of a woman to even waste my time. Not that I wasn't before, but I just didn't know my worth. My uncle once told me that my tongue was like a sword. I would have to agree, because I get scolded all the time by Garin about how I speak to him sometimes when I get angry. Now, though, I am more conscious of the words coming from my mouth. I will still chop you down with some words, but I have learned to use my mouth to explain my feelings, and my hands to pick up my pride and walk away. This has been a process that I had to get accustomed to. However, it's a safer outcome, because no one is suing me, I'm not going to jail, I don't have anyone filing restraining orders, and I'm not assaulting anyone or ending up with them assaulting me.

No man is worth jeopardizing my freedom or my self-respect. Back then, it just seemed so much easier to uphold the law of vengeance to get even. All the hurt and pain that I was put through…I just wanted the men to be able to experience some type of consequences. My road to find Mr. Right has led me down a path of Mr. Wrongs, and Mr. Right Nows. I don't have a fairytale ending to this, only the wisdom that came from all my mistakes. I take them and learn from them every day. I was hurt. I was angry. I was lashing out. I was scorned. I was battered. I was seeking out my own vengeance to get even. I was righting a wrong. That's all I can say to justify my behavior throughout this book. I now know that two wrongs equal a wrong.

I am a firm believer that everything happens for a reason. Sometimes you get put through things in your life to be able to share with someone else about your experiences. As you can see, I have experienced a lot. All of these stories are true. I wanted to share my story so that someone else could learn from my mistakes. I did things because I was angry and hurt. I have friends that say "I would never do this" or "I would never do that". Never say what you will or won't do, because you never know until you find yourself in that situation. I made a lot of mistakes in my journey. I know it seems like a lot of men, but I honestly never gave myself a break in between the relationships to heal and grow from each individual experience. Try not to judge too hard because sometimes it takes others a li'l longer to get themselves together. People who live in glass houses shouldn't throw stones. We're all a work still in progress. You may not agree with my choices in life, but it is my life, and it is already written.

Hopefully, by me sharing what I went through, you'll just know... No man is ever worth it. There is a saying that goes like this: you can mend a broken heart, but you can't mend a broken spirit. At the end of the day, there ain't no excuses, explanations, or apologies to any of these men for my actions. At the time I felt empowered for standing up for myself. I became a better me for me. However, I would like to thank all the men who have come and gone over the years for making my life experiences truly something unbelievable to talk about for years to come. Whether you impacted my life in a positive or negative way, I want to thank you for helping me become the person that I am supposed to be.

About the Author

Kennedee Devoe hails from Carson, CA, and currently resides in Los Angeles. She works in the nonprofit sector as a Program Director, and has a Master's Degree in Human Services.

Kennedee's Contact Information:

www.kdevoe.com

kennedeedevoe@yahoo.com

www.Facebook.com/kennedeedevoe

www.Twitter.com/kennedeedevoe

Instagram @ itmustbekd

www.youtube.com/kennedeedevoe

Spread the Word...Not the Book

Please recommend to family & friends, **available on Amazon, Kindle, Nook, Barnes & Noble, and local bookstores.**

Be sure to leave your review for this book on Amazon, Shelfari, Goodreads and Barnes & Noble.

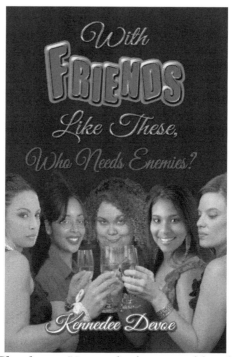

Check out Kennedee's second book

Coming February 7, 2014

Check out our services at
www.kdevoe.com

Made in the USA
San Bernardino, CA
31 July 2014